Mike Figgis

Digital Filmmaking

Mike Figgis is the renowned musician/filmmaker whose career began with the People Show in the 1970s. His film credits include *Stormy Monday*, *Internal Affairs*, and the award-winning *Leaving Las Vegas*, as well as the innovative digital films *Timecode* and *Hotel*. His photographs have been displayed at galleries, and he has created installations for gallery spaces.

by the same author

LEAVING LAS VEGAS
LOSS OF SEXUAL INNOCENCE
COLLECTED SCREENPLAYS 1
(STORMY MONDAY, LIEBESTRAUM, LEAVING LAS VEGAS)

PROJECTIONS 10 (EDITOR)

Digital
Filmmaking

Digital
Filmmaking

Mike Figgis

Faber and Faber, Inc.

An affiliate of Farrar, Straus and Giroux

New York

Faber and Faber, Inc.
An affiliate of Farrar, Straus and Giroux
19 Union Square West, New York 10003

Library of Congress Cataloging-in-Publication Data
Figgis, Mike.
    Digital filmmaking / Mike Figgis.
        p.   cm.
    ISBN-13: 978-0-571-22625-2 (pbk. : alk. paper)
    ISBN-10: 0-571-22625-6 (pbk. : alk. paper)
    1. Motion pictures—Editing—Data processing.   I. Title.

TR899.F48 2007
778.5'35—dc22

                                        2006102544

www.fsgbooks.com

1   3   5   7   9   10   8   6   4   2

Contents

Digital
Filmmaking

Introduction

I clearly remember the sense of frustration I felt when I began making films. I've always been fascinated by process, by how things *work*, and I've always asked questions. So I was hungry for information, but no-one would give it to me. I'd experienced a similar stonewall when I studied music. It seemed to me that the people who knew stuff weren't crazy about passing on that knowledge. The attitude seemed to be, 'That's for us to know and for you to guess.' So I resorted to bookshops, the sections on amateur filmmaking – 'How to Make a Super-8 Film' – and to magazines like *Amateur Photographer*.

Now that I think of it, the word 'amateur' isn't used very much any more. Nowadays everyone is a filmmaker. There is an interesting reason for this. Back in the day, there were two very big factors that separated the amateur from the pro: money and technology. An amateur filmmaker shot on Super-8, a pro shot on 16mm or 35mm. The difference in equipment and cost was huge. The price of a pro camera was prohibitive, and the cost of processing and post-production so high that only the very rich or the professionals could afford it. But that world has now vanished, and along with it the label 'amateur'.

I suppose I moved from amateur to pro status when I made my first film on 16mm. Then I began using 35mm. *Then* I began working in Hollywood. And I began to really understand how films were made by professionals. I have to say I wasn't very impressed.

There is a story about Orson Welles which may be true or may be urban myth, but in any case it contains a real truth. It goes like this. At the beginning of the *Citizen Kane* shoot Welles, whose background was 'hands-on' theatre, moved a light on the set. Greg Toland, the cinematographer, quietly told him that he shouldn't do that – the union regulation meant that a specific person and no-one else moved the lights. Welles then had lunch with Greg, who explained all these rules, and a few things more. (I imagine the gregarious Welles lapping up the information, asking lots of questions . . .) In later years Welles would always say that over the course of that lunch he learned everything he needed to know about filmmaking.

I buy that story. Because the truth is that making a film is very simple. What's complicated is the co-ordination of many simple elements, all of which need to be addressed at the same time. But the basics of filmmaking are not the same as the basics of brain surgery or rocket science. What I have tried to do in this book is lay out the basics and, in some instances, try to second-guess what might go wrong during the process, and then suggest ways of dealing with these problems.

Above all I want this to be a REALLY USEFUL BOOK. A long time ago I made a resolution with myself that I would never withhold any information that I possessed – I would always pass it on. I teach a lot these days, and I still try to do just that. There is enough information in this book to enable the reader to go out and make a film. The real test for anyone who wants to be a director is a different thing altogether: do you have the patience?

1
Choosing Your Weapon, Learning to Love It

Training the Eye

I got my first stills camera when I was eleven or twelve years old – and I've still got it. It was a point-and-shoot with a built-in flash. I think you got twelve shots per roll of film. I still print off that film today, and the quality is fantastic, because the negative is so big. There was one little switch that put a filter in front of the lens if the daylight was very bright – but pretty much all of my shots came out okay. If you think about the amount of time that directors of photography on movies spend with light meters . . . With your first camera, you just pointed it at something and took a photograph.

I then got hold of a very old 35mm camera, a Leica with a fixed lens – itself 35mm, fairly wide – and I shot some stuff on that. But it wasn't until I got a Nikon camera, and a long zoom lens, that I started taking portraits of people. If you take someone's portrait on a long lens, the subject is very sharp while everything in the background and foreground is soft. You start to get abstract shapes forming behind and in front of the subject. And suddenly you realise this is a whole different way of looking at things – an artificial way, because the eye doesn't function like that. And you realise these are the images you see in films – in war films, say, or any films that want to generate a kind of tension. You realise this is a particular 'look'. And you ask yourself: how do I get this look?

If you then start shooting film on a professional 16mm film camera such as the Aaton, and you get yourself a set of long lenses – well, the look you get when you gaze through the Aaton viewfinder is the same as what you got from the Nikon. Suddenly, as you shoot, you're connecting with the prospect of an image, with a 'look'. You sense that what you see is what you're going to get. And just by moving the focus ring, you start to get the power to control the image within the camera. So you begin to build up a kind of language of cinematography – and when you start writing descriptions of long-lens shots into your scripts, it shows you have a very clear idea of what you want the film to look like as you are writing it.

I came to these realisations as a result of having shot on a good 35mm stills camera, and then shooting 16mm film on the Aaton. And I would say that as part of your education as a filmmaker, the more time you spend with cameras the better it is for you. Whether it's a still camera, movie camera, digital camera, it's best to become so familiar with the camera that it becomes second nature to you. Every camera has a certain look and gives you a certain feel, and you begin to assimilate certain things unconsciously. Not only are you training your eye by how you use the camera, but you're developing an instinct for what it is you want to achieve. If you've achieved a certain effect through a stills camera, it's because you've made yourself familiar with that camera's mechanism. And if you know that's what you want, you can then take a digital camera and you can customise it in the same way – like making an extra limb for the camera.

Innovation by Accident

It was Sony, the great innovator, who came up with DAT – digital audio tape, a tiny but highly sophisticated tape. The first record-and-playback DAT machines were very well made, very robust, professional machines, not cheap but not fearfully expensive. And almost immediately the industry accepted it: DAT became *the* format for mastering sound. Certain engineers whom I talked to at the time were horrified. 'The quality's great, but where's your security? This is a tiny piece of tape in a plastic box . . .' – whereas before, you were using really big four-inch-wide master tapes. DAT wasn't invented as something to take over as the mastering format for recorded sound, but that's the way innovation works.

I feel the same thing has happened with video cameras, just because the domestic cameras now available are so good. For example, a reasonably priced DV camera that you buy in a store today is a better camera than an incredibly expensive hi-tech professional camera from ten years ago. There is no comparison in price. Technology has just moved on. Ten years ago the professional camera was entirely out of reach to anyone other than millionaires. And now we have these things that are almost disposable.

It's phenomenal – because up until this new digital era, the technology of film really had not shifted since the 1930s. It just became more sophisticated. Moviemaking technology was a lot like sewing-machine technology, and it worked fine – and continues to work fine. There had been no real breakthroughs – except, say, Dolby sound, or the invention of the Steadicam. Dolby was invented to deal with the inherent problem of hiss – white noise – on analogue tape. With digital technology we don't have analogue hiss any more, yet we've become addicted to the sound of Dolby, which is a certain kind of enhanced artificial sound. We accept that now as cinema sound, as 'reality'. It's not. But even though we don't really need Dolby technology any more, we're stuck with it. It's part of the deal if you make a film now.

A lot of the resistance to the new digital technology is coming from entrenched big business. In 2000 I shot a film called *Hotel* on four Sony PD100 digital cameras. But most people who saw it saw it projected as a 35mm print, and there were all kinds of problems in getting it on to 35mm – for instance, it had to project at a different speed from the speed I shot it. And it had to have Dolby sound on it. So at a certain point you have to ask: is the cart pulling the horse or the horse pulling the cart?

The Camera, Your Connection

By the late 1990s I had really welcomed the advent of digital equipment. I had tried it out and found it to be technically very interesting and good. I thought the new technology was something that would give a new vitality to the relationship between the director and the actors – to the whole filmmaking process – by radically reducing the number of people who needed to be on the set. It also gave great physical freedom to the actors, because they no longer had to concentrate on hitting specific floor marks for the sake of focus – instead it was possible to follow them wherever they went and not worry about lighting, because one could shoot digital in very low light situations. On automatic, the cameras adapt very quickly – and, in my opinion, perfectly satisfactorily – to a change in light conditions.

One of the problems in filmmaking, though, is that there is a certain snobbery about pieces of equipment. In the old days, when movie cameras were big and bulky and covered with strange knobs, there was a kind of automatic fear of the equipment – almost like being in the army – that would cause you to respect it in a certain way. That deference has gone now, and in a way I applaud its passing. But that said, what I'd like to reintroduce is the idea of a personal discipline towards the equipment.

These days a digital video camera might cost two or three hundred pounds and fit in the palm of your hand. The more accessible a camera seems – the smaller it is, the more plastic its component parts – the less respect it will be given. The standard reaction will be to treat it in a sloppy way. So I urge young filmmakers to change their attitudes about cameras. Don't have an attitude towards the equipment based on your preconception of its value. For the period of its working life, the camera will be the filmmaker's most crucial connection between the idea – the intention – and the result. That's the connection you're interested in. It's really important that you treat an inexpensive camera with exactly the same respect as you would an Arriflex 35mm camera. If it breaks and you need to throw it away, fine. But while it's functioning, it has to be treated with love and respect.

If that seriousness doesn't exist, if there's a disdainful or disrespectful attitude to the camera, then the result will not be as good. I would extend that philosophy all the way through the digital filmmaking process and for all the tools you use – the camera, the tape, the computer. These things are yours for the period of this creation, and they have all to be imbued with the correct significance and seriousness, as befits the filmmaking process. If they're not, then it will show.

I'll make an analogy with music. If you go to a concert and hear a really great violinist playing a Stradivarius, you'll be witness to a magnificent sound and a great performance. Now that violinist could take a twenty-dollar Chinese violin made for schoolchildren, tune it and play it, and I guarantee a lot of people couldn't tell the difference from the Stradivarius – because of the musician. Similarly, a great drummer can pick up a wooden packing case and make it sound like an amazing set of drums. A photographer – let's say a Cartier-Bresson – could pick up a Kodak Brownie and without a doubt he'd take great photographs. The point is that it doesn't really matter what the equipment is. It really matters who the artist is, and what their attitude is. So a serious filmmaker will pick up an Arriflex, 16mm or 35mm, or a Panasonic video camera, and you will see immediately that there is a serious intention in the way they're holding the camera and the way they're recording the image. It will not be ambiguous. It will not be negotiable. It will not be in doubt. They will state their relationship to the camera, like the musician and the violin, the drummer and the packing case. The way that you pick up a camera and the way that you address the camera is fundamental.

It's more than just keeping the camera well tuned. When you take something out of a box which is going to be the connection between you and your artistic vision, unless you then establish a specific kind of relation with it – turn it from an object into an extension of yourself – then I don't think you can call yourself a filmmaker. Nor can you really hope to get the best results.

Due Diligence

The first thing a soldier is taught is how to dismantle his gun and put it back together – make sure it's clean, make sure it functions – because that's the thing that will save his life. You don't want your gun to jam. You don't want your camera to jam either. If something goes wrong with it, you want to know how to fix it or adapt it. That's why I always say it's important to own your camera, because in that way you have a different relationship to it.

I once loaned out a camera that I'd looked after for four years. It came back to me and the front of the lens-mount was broken off. I rang the people who borrowed it and they said, 'Oh yeah, we noticed that. We put it back on again. We thought it was okay . . .' I knew that camera well enough. The only way the mount could have broken off was if someone had picked it up by the front end and treated it roughly. If you owned it, you would never treat it that way.

In 1995 I bought a new Aaton Super-16mm film camera, my second such camera. It was very expensive, and I was about to shoot my first film with it. I went with a DP and a camera assistant on a recce around Soho, just to shoot some stuff with available light at night. I ended up in the Groucho Club having a cup of coffee. And I remember looking down at my feet and seeing that the camera assistant had put my brand new Aaton on to the tile floor of the restaurant and had gone off to the toilet, leaving the camera unattended. And the Groucho Club is full of drunks . . . When he came back I said, 'What are you doing?' And he said, 'Oh, it seemed okay there.' I think he felt like Super-16 somehow wasn't to be treated with the reverence of 35mm. I was really shocked.

When shooting *Hotel* entirely on DV-Cam I was equally shocked that sometimes the camera assistants didn't bother to check the camera in between takes for spit marks on the lens. If you're shooting on video sometimes you will be three or four inches away from an actor's face while they're talking, and inevitably they're going to spray the lens with little bits of saliva. Projected on to a screen, those small things turn into golf balls. And seeing these huge marks on the lens, I went completely ballistic.

Here is my advice: as soon as the camera's given back to you, once you've finished shooting, don't just put it down and get a cup of coffee. Look at that camera lovingly, and go through every function on it, every possibility – the battery, the lens, all the things that could go wrong.

The other crucial thing about getting to know your camera is that it is your job to shoot things *continually* – particularly on video, because it doesn't cost you any money – in order to try things, different combinations of things, and then look at the results immediately and make notes. Consult the manual that comes with the camera, and then start customising it to your own particular needs. These days, if you just accept a camera as it comes out of the box, you will get a totally acceptable result, technically. But whether that's enough to satisfy you aesthetically is another matter. It wouldn't be enough for me.

When you take it out of the box and you open the instructions, you start to absorb the information that the manufacturers think you should know through their book. I always start a little notebook for this process. I spend a couple of days deconstructing the menu, just toying, saying to myself, 'Okay, it says here if I do this then this will happen.' So I try it and I think, 'Well that's interesting. They don't mention this particular combination, so I'll try that too, and make a note.' Maybe I end up thinking, 'Oh, I see, if you do this and this and this, it means you can shoot at very slow shutter speed, plus you can change the aperture to make a very high-contrast black and white image. Which means you can virtually shoot in the dark.' In this way I've discovered what is an interesting combination of settings for me, and it becomes my personal menu.

Fidelity to Your Favourite

I remember Francis Coppola, years ago, envisaging a kind of cinema where by use of electrodes you could somehow use your own brain and eyes as the camera . . . What's interesting about cinema is this process of having to go through the medium of the camera: it becomes the extension of your eye and your hand and your creative process. So whenever I've bought a new camera I've also tried to limit – not always successfully – the number of cameras I'm using at any given time. It's almost like I don't want to dilute my concentration through the camera, particularly now when there are so many products on the market.

I used to feel sorry for people like David Bailey who were constantly inundated with product. Olympus or Canon or

Nikon or Leica would give him all these cameras. And you can see a slightly hopeless look on certain photographers' faces as they're surrounded by this barrage of equipment and they think, 'Which one? Do I use the Leica? The Hasselblad?' In terms of stills cameras I myself have always struggled between that temptation and the voice that says, 'Actually this is my favourite camera . . .' For a period of fifteen years I just used a Leica and none other, except a Hasselblad for very formal portraits. And I had a very happy relationship with the Leica, which only came to an end when I decided to move over to digital. At which point I tried lots of different cameras and found one that seemed fantastic – partly because the process is suddenly so personal, whereas with the Leica I always had to go to a laboratory to get my stuff processed.

I've had the same experience with movie cameras. Once, in Los Angeles, someone loaned me the then-latest Sony camera, the PD100. And I immediately liked it. I liked the design, which is unusual for me. I thought everything about the camera was interesting. The results were amazing. So I bought several of them to shoot *Hotel* and I have, up until very recently, just used that camera. Despite the fact that Canon and JVC brought out interesting cameras, and there were cameras that were perhaps more technically evolved, I didn't want a confusion of equipment. I wanted the ability to focus on one camera. If I had a lot of different cameras, I know that just because of the way my brain works I would get confused between one camera and another. Whereas I knew exactly why this PD100 was good for me, and in any given working situation I could set it up and adjust it very quickly. *That* was perfectly good enough for me.

2
Excursions into Super-8, 16mm, Super-16 and Hi-8

Opening Shots

It was 1980. I had been working for ten years with a performance group called the People Show, and I had become convinced that they should get involved with film. But they weren't interested, so I decided to leave. I thought I would go to the National Film School, but I didn't get in. One of the reasons was because I was honest and told the School that my film experience to that point had been entirely with Super-8. As part of my desire to start experimenting with film at the tail end of the People Show, I had bought myself a Super-8 camera, a Canon 512.

I really liked the design of that camera. It was very simple, silent, battery-operated. It had a zoom and a kind of pistol-grip, which folded up in order to put the camera away. That grip felt almost like holding a gun. Guns are designed in a certain way so that people can shoot and kill, and that design also has to consider what is the steadiest way to hold the gun so that your shot will hit the target. You can draw an analogy here with camera design. The pistol grip on this Canon 512 was very, very stable. You held the camera in your right hand, and your forefinger was on the trigger that started and stopped it.

The problem with Super-8 is that the strip of film itself is tiny, which leaves an even tinier strip for sound recording.

And given the limitations in editing – which was already fiddly, and almost impossible if, like me, you had big hands – it seemed to me that the resultant sound quality really wasn't good enough to be bothered with. I became interested in film because I was interested in sound. I always loved movies because I liked listening to the soundtracks in the cinema – to the *size* of the sound. I wasn't interested in being a film director; I was passionate about sound.

By then I was making very complicated sound tapes using recorders, loops and state-of-the-art sound technology – analogue sound, but very high quality. For example, I was among the first people who used a portable mixer – this was twenty-five years ago. So I evolved a method whereby I shot Super-8 films silently, and made the soundtracks separately. And that philosophy has stayed with me.

What really thrilled me about Super-8 was that you could shoot a film, then get it back from the lab a week or so later, and project it. The quality of the image was very grainy, the colours were very high-contrast – reds were very red. The colour rendition was impressionistic, but still far more satisfying than anything that was available with early video cameras. So, from an aesthetic point of view, with Super-8 you immediately got a result that was representational but also interestingly removed from reality – you were looking at something that had a kind of richness and artistic potential to it. For example, if you shot in very low light, the grain structure was really interesting. And if you shot with an electric light bulb everything went very yellow. You very quickly learnt certain rules about bright sunlight, overcast light, shooting at night, shooting with artificial light . . . You started to factor these kinds of things into your idea of shooting something before you actually shot it.

The cameras weren't cheap, but they were within a modest price range if you saved up. The film stock was 'process-paid'. You bought a plastic cassette, you popped it in the camera – there was no threading, it was very convenient, like videotape – and the cassette, running at eighteen frames a second, gave you between four and five minutes of film time. Then, when it came to an end, you popped it into a yellow envelope that came with your package, which had an address in Hemel Hempstead, you sent it off with your address on the back, and about a week later the processed film came back to you on a spool and you could throw it on to a projector and watch it. So there was a delay between shooting the film and seeing the results, but that created a real tension in itself. For example, there was nothing more disappointing than getting back this thing for which you'd paid to be processed, and it would be blank or completely overexposed. As I remember it, each cassette cost £3 or £4. At that point I really couldn't afford to buy a lot of stock, so you already had the idea that this was a very precious five minutes. The way you'd shoot the film would be entirely governed by that consideration. No shot would last longer than 15 seconds – that would be a very long take. You might have the cassette in your camera for a couple of weeks, unused.

Initially, the first things you shoot with a movie camera come from the joy of having that camera and pulling a trigger and getting images, of anything from flowers to kids to waterfalls – all the things that, traditionally, all over the world, people want to film. A lot of the material that I'd shot was of my family, my kids, and I put things together for them, almost like a family album, but in the form of a film.

Once I had mastered how the camera worked, I immediately wanted to start making sequential narrative films. So I made children's films while I was on holiday in Spain. I made one called *Kidnapped* with my kids and two very strange-looking Spanish twins. They kidnapped my son, Arlen, who at that time was about eighteen months old, and he was rescued by my seven-year-old stepdaughter Romany. I started being confronted by questions such as: how you do fake flying? Say you want someone to jump off what looks like a very high wall. So you find a very high wall, you make a wide shot, you see Romany run up to the edge at the top and look down – a 40-foot drop. Then you find another stretch of wall that's lower but looks very similar, and shoot a close-up of her jumping off, and then a close-up of her landing. Then you'd go back to the wide shot. Then you would cut the sequence together, and it worked.

So, immediately, I had started thinking of sequences and how to realise them. With that in mind I would – not exactly storyboard – but I would make shot-lists. To make *Kidnapped*, which is probably a 5-minute film, I used two Super-8 cassettes, about 9 minutes of film. The ratio was pretty frugal. But it really forced me to actually work out what I wanted to do. Rather than the situation which now exists – and, perversely, is quite intimidating for young filmmakers – where you can get hold of relatively cheap equipment that takes 60- or 90-minute cassettes.

Later in my career, when I had the luxury of shooting on Super-16, I'd constantly get phone calls from film students asking if I had any short ends. These are the bits left over from shooting a proper film, maybe a hundred feet here and there, which you would put in light-tight labelled cans. And you'd give them to film students, and they would shoot their student movies on them, because the price of stock and processing was so expensive. Today, though, in the digital age, the concept of film stock being precious is no longer an issue. With analogue tape – the format that pre-ceded digital – you could reuse it but you might get 'print-through', because it's a technically different form of recording. With digital tape, because it's digital informa-tion, once you wipe it, you really do wipe it. So you can reuse digital stock over and over again without any real fear of an aberration appearing on the tape or the recorded image. I would say, though, that too much information and too much choice is in itself a huge limitation on creativity. Also, because stock isn't limited nowadays, the discipline of thinking ahead doesn't always occur to people – they just shoot and shoot.

The main reason I moved over from Super-8 was that I wanted a strong, punchy image for the audience to watch, and at that time Super-8 didn't really give you that possibil-ity. It's to do with the amount of hot light you have to pass through an image in order to get a strong projection. As we've said, the size of a Super-8 frame is tiny. The amount of heat you need on the bulb to get a big throw from an 8mm projector means that if the film sticks even for a moment then it immediately burns the frame out. That can happen on 16mm as well, but not with the same frequency.

Another problem was that because Super-8 was an ama-teur gauge, you were always working with your originals. In other words, you shot reversal stock, not negative, and sent it off to Kodak, who would process it and then send the same piece of celluloid back to you, only this time with a positive image on it. Thus, every time you projected the film you were scratching it. And you didn't have a separate original. Eventually, realising how vulnerable I was in this way, I found a small cottage company who would make copies of my edited originals for me, and I would use the copies to project. There would be a generation loss, but that was okay because the images were not crystal clear to start off with.

Moving On to 16mm

In 1980 I did a performance-art theatre piece called *Redheugh*, in which I incorporated a 40-minute film shot on 16mm – my first long film. But I used a camerawoman, Diane Tammes, to shoot it, so I wasn't personally involved with the camera – though I was watching all the time and trying to absorb as much information as possible. But that film represented a transition for me from Super-8 to 16mm. In that transition, you increase the size of the negative. 16mm is a nice size for cutting. You can hold it up and see the image. From a tactile point of view, it was something that had a bit more substance to it. The editing machinery was much more sophisticated. 16mm and Super-16 was technically a very evolved system using Steenbeck flatbed editing machines. It functioned as a kind of mini-version of 35mm using exactly the same technology – at least in the UK, though this wasn't the case in America.

Once I felt I was ready to shoot on 16mm, I bought a camera called an Arriflex ST, which was made just after the

Second World War. It was battery-operated, but you wore a battery belt. Relatively speaking, though, it was a small camera, with a triple-lens mount. You often see it in old newsreel footage; it's the model all the news people used. You could put a 400-foot magazine on top of it or a 100-foot load inside. It also had a vari-speed. You were supposed to do light readings, guess the aperture, but there was no way of checking anything. And it was a silent camera; you couldn't shoot sync sound. But I wasn't interested in shooting sound on camera at that time.

I bought the camera and went to New York on a budget ticket to shoot material for a performance piece called *Animals of the City*, commissioned by a theatre in Paris. In New York I had so many boxes of equipment that I couldn't pick them all up by myself. But every day I went out with my camera. I decided that I wanted aerial footage of New York, so I bought a ticket on a tourist helicopter. This aerial tour was about fifteen minutes. Because the Arriflex was a four-minute load, I knew I'd have to change the film while I was in the helicopter. So the night before, I took a roll of blank film and practised changing the magazine in the dark. Unlike with Super-8, you had to take off the side of the Arriflex, take out the film, put it into a light-tight tin, and put that in your pocket. Then you had to unwrap a new roll, open the gate on the camera, thread the film on to a take-in spool, turn it through to make some tension, run a little bit to make sure it was in the right teeth, put the top back on again, and then continue filming.

So I had my Arriflex and also my Super-8 camera and a stills camera, all in a soft bag. I was wearing a thick tweed coat because it was very cold. What I hadn't factored in at all was that there would be other people in the helicopter – in fact, it was absolutely crammed full of Japanese tourists. The heating system in this helicopter came straight from the engine, so it pumped in a lot of hot air. And within two minutes of taking off, I was sweating so much that I could feel the coat getting wet. When I finally got out of the helicopter, the coat had doubled in weight. I hogged the window, which was appalling behaviour because the other tourists had paid money and wanted to see out of the window too . . . But I managed to get quite a lot of footage of New York from the air. Then I went out filming at two in the morning on 42nd Street and managed to film myself being hit by three youths walking towards me. As they came close I was thinking, 'What a great shot! I wonder when they're going to part in front of me?' At the last minute a fist came in and whammed the camera against my face . . . I sent the rolls of film off for processing, having no idea whether I'd got the exposure right or not. But that was my first experience with 16mm.

Then I was commissioned to do a very complicated performance-art piece in Amsterdam. I persuaded the producer to lend me some money, and with that money I bought an Aaton Super-16 camera. That allowed me to film for the first time with sound. I had no idea how to use it, but I bought the camera and a set of lenses, and I turned up in Amsterdam with the manual.

The Aaton offered the possibility – just by changing a very small piece of metal – of shooting either standard 16mm or Super-16. Standard-16 is a TV format, which is, let us say, square. Super-16 is the same format as 35mm, a rectangle. With 16mm you don't record sound on the actual film, you have to use a synchronised tape recorder. The speed at which the Aaton exposed film was accurate to the nearest frame, so that when a tape recorder ran at the same time using a pulse, the two would stay in sync with each other. The way the Aaton was able to adjust to a wider frame for Super-16 was simply this: in a piece of film held up to the light there are sprocket holes on both the left and the right, but Aaton realised that you only need sprocket holes on one side of the film, giving you more of the strip to play with, and they utilised that freed-up space to create a wider oblong frame. To record sync sound I adapted a professional Sony cassette recorder, and that worked well.

When you shoot you find a big difference between 35mm and 16mm or Super-16, because of the size of the negative in relation to the lenses that you're using. The depth of field – the ability of the camera to hold everything in focus, which you get more of with 16mm – also presents a stylistic difference. One of the criticisms Jean-Luc Godard offers of digital technology is that the image has such depth of field that it's not a filmic look for him – he finds that a limitation. To which I would say, 'All these things can be dealt with.'

The problem is most video cameras work on an automatic function: light hits the lens and carries through to a sensor, which works out the exposure automatically. If you want to cut down the exposure and narrow the depth of field, then you have to put grey-scale neutral density filters in front of the lens. They don't change the colour of anything; they just start blocking the amount of light getting into the lens, so widening the aperture and shortening the depth of field. Every camera has a natural tendency, depending on its mechanical structure. If you delve into that mechanical structure, there's usually a way to bypass it in order to get the effect you want. So part of the filmmaking process is to understand the basic technology that you're dealing with, in order to come up with ways of customising the equipment to get the result that you want.

Video: The Early Cameras

When I began to shoot on Super-8 I would buy amateur film magazines. Even though the articles were quite banal, there were snippets of technical information I found I could use. About this time, the first video cameras were hitting the market, and these magazines would report on them, initially with some scorn – 'This will never take over from Super-8, the quality isn't very good.' Then, quite quickly, these video cameras started to get more editorial space, and there came a point where they began to be taken seriously.

The first video cameras that I saw in the '70s in America were reel-to-reel – they used a system very like the original tape-recorders. But the recording facility wasn't onboard the camera, so you recorded straight on to a tape machine via a big fat cable. Eventually people got the idea that you needed to record on cassette, in a compartment on the camera.

When video first hit the market domestically there were two systems, both cassette-based: Betamax, originated by Sony, and VHS, made by Philips. There was also U-Matic, but that was strictly for the professional market, for television. The Beta system was a slightly smaller and more robust cassette, but with a wider tape. Beta didn't work in the domestic market and it was phased out, but it continued in the professional market, and Sony stayed with that design for their Beta SP and then Digi-Beta systems. But at the time VHS was the domestic winner, so when the first consumer cameras came out, they were huge. The VHS tape alone was bigger than most cameras are now. And the cameras were very bulky and, aesthetically, really ugly. I should say I'm still a complete snob about camera design. As with cars, you want something that looks like it's going to be around for more than six months. Plastic always has a shine when you buy it, and then after a year it looks very dull, or bits have broken off, or it's cracked. It doesn't inspire the idea of permanence or any kind of long life. And as for the image – if you look, for example, at the VHS home movies that are part of *Capturing the Friedmans*, the quality is very blurry, the colours bleed, the reds are a nightmare. That was typical of VHS. To me, the image had no appeal at all. So even the facts that you had a portable camera and the ability to shoot long takes didn't occur to me as being particularly interesting, because the end result looked unattractive.

Then in 1985 I was on tour with *Animals of the City*, which turned out to be the last of the performance pieces that I did. My sound technician was an Australian guy called Kim, and he was a complete Super-8 fanatic who would film everywhere we went. He was also a obsessive reader of magazines about amateur filmmaking, and I remember a conversation where he said: 'Have you heard about this new format that Sony are coming out with? It's a complete revolution. Basically, if you imagine an audio-cassette tape, Sony are coming out with a version of that for video, even smaller, and it's called Hi-8. It's a tiny tape and they're designing cameras especially for it and the quality is going to be a complete breakthrough.'

Hi-8 was released nine months later. By then I was already making feature films, and I owned 16mm cameras. But I was beginning to be intrigued by the idea of owning a decent video camera – for the reason that still attracts me to it, namely the ability to shoot something and see it back straight away and not have to spend extra money going to laboratories and having to deal with technicians who are struggling to translate your ideas.

In 1989 when I was working on my second American feature, *Liebestraum*, I put forward a proposal to MGM to make a documentary about making this film. I knew they would spend money promoting *Liebestraum*, so I thought, 'If they give *me* the money to make the documentary I could buy a professional Hi-8 camera.' In fact, they didn't agree, but I decided to go ahead anyway. My first Hi-8 was a broadcast camera, really quite big, with a professional lens on the front. I shot hours of footage of the making of *Liebestraum*; I never turned this into a documentary, but that was my first experience with video. Meanwhile Sony's success with Hi-8 made all the other major manufacturers of video equipment realise that you could make a camera with a smaller cassette that could still be a professional format.

Size, Miniaturisation and Stability

The evolution of the video camera springs from the microchip revolution and the attendant concept of ever-increasing miniaturisation. If you opened up an early consumer video camera, you would see that it was full of little screws and printed circuits and pieces of coloured wire going from one place to another. Open up a digital camera today and you won't see any of that – other than the little boards. It's analogous to the early mobile phones, which could have killed you if someone hit you with them. Now the phones are so small you almost have to move them between your mouth and your ear. The same thing happened to the video cameras, and to stills cameras, to a point where you had to start asking: has the camera become too small?

What had principally held back film camera design were the mechanical components of the camera. They were a certain size, they were metal, and they were a certain weight, because they had to support relatively large pieces of film. 35mm has a bulk that is unique. If you want to shoot more than three minutes without changing the magazine, you're talking about a huge amount of weight and bulk that has to be housed in lightproof, weatherproof housings, which then also has to clip on to the camera. And the camera has to have a transport system that will support the rather large, clumsy celluloid. That was the limitation. The minute you get rid of the need to have celluloid and the housing and all the rest of it, you completely liberate the design of the camera. It became clear that using digital technology and very small pieces of tape meant the housing for the recording could be very small, the lens could be very small, and so on. It suddenly seemed like a really good idea to make everything tiny. So there was a period of design where the market was flooded by miniaturised cameras.

That first professional Sony Hi-8 that I bought had a good design, in that the basic chassis was heavy enough that it sat solidly on your shoulder and it required two hands to operate it. In that way, stability of the image took care of itself. In fact, it was quite hard to wobble the camera. Even if you were hand-holding it as you walked, its weight and your body were well-balanced. I used that camera to start shooting documentaries. One of these was about William Forsythe and the Frankfurt ballet, a very avant-garde ballet company, so the way the dancers moved was very unpredictable – they improvised all the time. Sometimes there would be thirty-five dancers or more on stage, and very often they danced with their eyes closed. If they hit the camera they could really hurt themselves.

So when I was moving and filming these dancers, I had to be very aware of the unpredictability of their movements. And I started to think this camera was too heavy for the job in hand. Another problem with the camera was that it didn't have a display screen – I always had to look through the viewfinder. But I discovered that if I flipped the lid of the viewfinder open, what was revealed was a tiny little monitor about an inch by an inch, black and white, but quite bright. And the eyepiece itself was on a swivel, like that of a film camera, so that you could rotate the eyepiece for the comfort of where your body was. So I could hold the camera with my right hand, and with the viewfinder lid flipped open I could see this monitor and even pivot myself around it. Because I didn't have to have the camera glued to my eye, it meant that my head was free while I was shooting, all the better to check out where the other dancers were. I was suddenly liberated, in the sense that if I could see someone doing something interesting while I was shooting one dancer, then I could move over to the other dancer.

It was still a heavy camera, and by the end of the second

month of shooting I felt as if I'd been going to the gym – my shoulders had become stronger, but very sore. But I knew by now that this camera was too heavy. So I invested in an early DV camera, the first of the mini DVs, Sony's VX1000. It still didn't have a screen, but it was small enough that the ability to manoeuvre it wasn't an issue. And the image quality was excellent. Once, when I was visiting Cuba, I looked at some stuff done by documentary filmmakers who had just gone out and shot in beautiful light in the jungle. I turned to one of the tutors and said, 'Was this shot on 16mm or 35mm?' And they said, 'No, this was actually shot on a VX1000.'

What I started to notice straight away, though, was that the camera was very light. I didn't realise it while I was shooting – you can't really judge it in the moment – but I realised when I looked at what I'd shot that the camera was flying away in small ways while I was holding it. It was designed to be held with one hand pushed through a strap, which was fine if you were standing still and shooting only a quick shot. But if you're shooting a documentary in takes of 15 to 20 minutes and you want to keep fluid, your hand became trapped in the strap, and when you tried to remove it the camera wobbled and you got a very unstable, aesthetically unsatisfying result.

In fact, all of the little illustrations in the manual for the camera encouraged you to use just one hand to operate it. Because of the design, people are reluctant to put two hands on the camera – they feel it's superfluous. But there's a simple principle here – the smaller the camera in relation to the size of your hand, the greater will be the exaggeration caused by any movement of your hand. I make the analogy of a waiter with a huge tray of glasses filled with water: if he holds the tray with one hand in the middle, any movement of his hand might cause it to tip and spill, but not if he grasps both edges, because in the event of any wobble then one hand will compensate for the other. If you're holding something from the centre of gravity, you can't compensate.

When I go on holiday I find it wonderful to be able to fold up my video camera and put it in my pocket – knowing that I don't need a flight case to carry my camera any more. But when you actually come to shoot, the end result may be distorted and wobbly – because the camera's too small. This is an important lesson, because filmmakers need to train themselves when they're shooting not to think only about the camera in the present tense but also about the image in the future tense – when it's really big and thrown up on to a screen.

These days I see people operating digital cameras with one hand, holding a mobile phone with the other, smoking a cigarette . . . It irritates me in a similar way to people driving power-steering cars with one hand. Why wouldn't you want to drive with two hands, if you are driving with four people in the car and you could kill them in an instant? Video cameras are designed so that if you look at the viewfinder the image looks stable. It's only when you blow up the image that you start dealing with motion sickness – watching the film can literally make people sick because of the unsteady operating. Another problem is that the success of the Dogme 95 movement made it chic to wobble the camera – one of the characteristics of Lars von Trier's films is spasmodic camera work. And while one can see, intellectually, where he's coming from, it hasn't been a good influence on people coming up in digital filmmaking, because they think that is acceptable. For me, it gets totally in the way of the narrative, because one is too aware of the camera.

This problem in digital cinema of sloppy movement and lack of horizontal stability on the camera led me to design a piece of equipment specifically to deal with that problem of the camera being too small to hold steady. It forces the operator to be more stable and less wobbly – with some considerable degree of success.

3
Customised Cameras, Video Aesthetics

Operating

Before I came to film, my background was performance and music, so I was reared on the idea that whatever I did creatively, I would have a direct relationship with my audience. With the People Show, once you go on stage, bang, there's an immediate response from the audience. And you're able to capitalise immediately on that response and compound it. The same applies to playing live music.

Then I started making films . . . and I realised that your role as a director puts you many steps removed from this possibility of an instant response. You do a lot of pre-planning, you set it all up, but then you kind of watch from an angle. And the main relationship from that point takes place between the camera person and the actors. I found that very frustrating, because it knocked out my ability to react quickly to a situation and to impose my creative energy directly on to the actors, just because there was always this time lag. On top of that, the sheer numbers of people you had to deal with – all of whom feel they're in first position in terms of their need for your time and attention – often meant that your creative juices were constantly being interrupted.

So in 1995 when I shot *Leaving Las Vegas* on Super-16, I started to operate the camera on a sort of fifty-fifty basis with the Director of Photography, or DP, Declan Quinn, and immediately felt like I'd got back my connection with

33

the actors. Until that point, because of the way cinema production is geared, I had grudgingly accepted the argument that goes: 'Okay, the good news is you're the director and it's a terrific job, the bad news is you just have to accept a slight time-lag in your creative process.' It *is* the case that a director has to be someone who can anticipate situations in a certain way, and I believe I can do so, but I think I'm more useful and more creative when I have a more immediate connection with what's going on. So, from *Leaving Las Vegas* onwards, I tried to make it my business to always be operating in some form. That was possible on any Super-16 project, but not on 35mm.

On digital projects, operating suddenly became not only possible, but it was almost as if I *knew* as much about digital cinematography as anybody else. In fact, in some instances, more, because I was inventing bits and bobs to make the process more fluid. And because I had access to the equipment all the time, I was in a position where I could think about it practically and physically, even when the filmmaking process wasn't happening. I'd just take out the camera and adapt it in some way and think about what little gizmos I could put on it to make it more efficient. Certainly with documentaries I was shooting it myself, with maybe two or three other cameramen as well. In 1999 I made a film called *Timecode*: we had four cameras and I shot one of them. In 2000 I made *Hotel*: again four cameras and I shot one of them, and I ended up shooting most of that myself.

Interestingly, on *Hotel* I had three other camera people, and sometimes I would find myself feeling bad and saying to them: 'Okay, why don't you go and shoot this or that?' In fact I was trying to be fair to the crew rather than to my instinct, which was to go and shoot it all myself – because I knew exactly what I wanted, and I wouldn't have to explain it either, so ultimately it would save time. And saving that time affected a transformation. If you've got a group of on-the-ball actors, the speed at which you can set up a shot is much quicker than if I'd had to explain to a crew what I wanted, where the lights needed to be, and all the rest of it. You can see it all yourself very, very quickly. You just look around and get yourself into a position where the light's going to work – and you know it will, because you can see it on the monitor – then you quickly rehearse with the actors and jump straight into shooting.

The Importance of Being Oneself

The film business has always been a war between individual creativity on the part of filmmakers, and studios who see their job as being to curtail creativity and control it themselves. They always talk about a team when in fact it's a dictatorship. Very benevolent, but despotic. The more control producers can have over score, camera movement, casting, story and so on, the more secure they are in a very insecure business. So, the more we talk about guerrilla filmmaking and individuals, I think the healthier it is, even though that may also produce some monumentally awful egos. But at least it allows for the possibility of a single creative voice, which is the source of all creativity.

Any period of technological innovation in cinema will create its own crop of specific egos – whether it's Godard or Lars von Trier or Harmony Korine or me or whoever . . . We all have to have egos in order to push forward ideas. We're all dogmatic in our own way. We think we're not, but we are. And the digital video era also created a certain irony – Godard, for instance, fought so hard down the years for the sorts of benefits to filmmakers that these cameras have brought in, and then, when the technology suddenly becomes, as it were, available on the high street, his natural kind of intellectual snobbery slams down the shutters and he says, in effect: 'No. I'm going to use video, but I'm going to shoot really old-fashioned U-Matic or Beta-SP' – or whatever ghastly-looking thing he used to shoot *Éloge de l'amour* (2001). It's as if at a certain point he just lost interest, because it was too accessible, no longer an exclusive thing – and Godard is all about exclusive filmmaking. And while that may distance him from other people, in his case, I think it's important that such aloofness exists.

All art forms have their own elitism and exclusivity within them. Anybody can buy a pencil and paper, but not everybody can draw. The next level of discrimination is: what kind of paper are you using? We've always been interested in the materials that have gone into a really interesting piece of work. And for those who maybe can't do it that well, become almost obsessive about the paper and the pencil, and start writing whole articles about materials.

So within the generic availability of digital video, I do think it's important for us to create our own systems. It may be egalitarian, this idea that you can go to the high street and buy a camera and be the same as everybody else – but it's not very sexy. We want to have a Leica because that makes us part of a really exclusive club, with our own badge. It's like press photographers in war zones – they buy a Nikon or Canon and then they blank out the manufacturer's logo with a piece of gaffer tape. I've always wondered why. I think it's a way of saying, 'This isn't a Nikon, this is *my* camera.' It seems important for us that we buy something generic and then we modify it. We drill a hole in it that makes it different. Me, I cut the strap off a video camera, and that makes it a Mike Figgis camera because I've disabled it in a specific way. But there are other little things that I will do to the camera that will make it immediately a Mike Figgis camera, and that will limit it – but, I think, in a good way, by forcing me to treat the camera in a certain way. In fact, I designed a rig called the Fig-Rig, which has its own built-in limitations but which, I hope, will make for better results in terms of the way people use cameras.

Shaky-Cam: The Wobble, Its Uses and Abuses

I shoot on video because it gives me freedom as a filmmaker to try new things. However, I would still like the result to be watchable – unless I'm deliberately trying to make it wobbly, as in *The Blair Witch Project*, which gives a sense of a point of view that is very fragile and sometimes terrified. That's a perfectly honourable technique; even on 35mm there have always been attempts to try to distort the camera movements to convey that sense of a vulnerable POV.

If, say, you're a diehard Dogme filmmaker, you might want to stay with the wobble – it's a stylistic choice. It's almost like the trad jazz revival in the '50s in Britain, where certain bands deliberately played out of tune to give an authentic New Orleans sound. Hence the phrase, when you are tuning up with musicians: 'It's close enough for jazz.' Meaning it doesn't really matter if you're in tune or not. In fact, it might sound more believable if you're slightly out. So that's your choice. It's not mine. And one of the factors that is limiting the ability of the new films made digitally to get into a wider market is a perception among the mainstream distribution people that digital filmmaking is somehow synonymous with being wobbly, meaning cheap, and that it turns the audience off.

In 2000 I made a decision to buy the Sony PD100 and to shoot *Hotel* entirely with that camera. I quickly prioritised the issue of stability with this camera. I wasn't satisfied with it handheld. I didn't want to put the cameras on tripods – that would have defeated the whole point of having them. I wanted them to be very flexible, very mobile – in fact, I wanted to design a system where one could really get the best out of the possibility of recording sound with the camera. And so in pre-production, while I was still in London, I began to explore the idea of constructing some kind of rig that these cameras could live on, which would also support additional equipment – for sound and so on. That way, I could make the person who was traditionally called the Director of Photography, the DP, also the person recording the sound.

The camera itself only offered an onboard microphone. So I went to the back pages and small ads of *American Cinematographer* magazine and I started to look at what was available on the market specifically for these cameras. I discovered that you could buy equipment that gave you the possibility of using professional sound recording equipment that could very easily screw into the bottom of the camera. There was a little box called a Beech Tech that had two XLR plug sockets on the side, one pot for the left-hand channel and another for the right, so you could control the input of two professional microphones – or one could also be a radio mic. Already that was a huge improvement, technically, on what the camera offered. The onboard microphone could be bypassed and you would have a digital audio recording system, giving the operator control of left and right channels.

But for that control to be meaningful I still needed to be able to monitor the sound while I was recording it. I then discovered that the same company who made this little box also made a display unit that gave you an LED read-out of your recording, with a red peak-meter, so that if your sound was distorting it would show as red. Now, in order to do this, the camera had to be set up quite delicately on a day-to-day basis. As a little ritual, you had to balance the input with the output by going into the internal menu of the camera. It was fiddly but it was possible. And it meant that, at a stroke, by buying and testing these little bits of equipment, you had taken the camera out of automatic-expensive-amateur status into manual-inexpensive-professional status.

But I still had a problem with stability. Then, through one of my sons, I heard about a young designer called Ben Wilson at the Royal College of Art who had been focusing on the design of push-bikes for disabled children. These were bikes where you controlled the direction in which you were going not by using handlebars, but by using body weight – shifting it to the left or the right. So I invited Ben to come in for a cup of coffee and told him what I wanted was some kind of rig for the camera that would deal with stability. He agreed that this would be an interesting thing. He was also a skateboarder, and an amateur cameraman – I say 'amateur', but those terms don't really apply any more. Let's say, like a lot of young guys, he was making films . . .

I invited him to come in on a regular basis for a couple of weeks, and he'd turn up with a tape measure and gaffer tape and various clamps and pieces of tubular metal. And what we would do was bend certain shapes. I'd originally worked on the idea of anchoring the weight in something like a triangle – as you see in marches and parades when people are walking with flags on poles. The flagpole is very heavy, but they're wearing a belt with a socket in it, and the flag sits in that so that the weight is being distributed on to the hips and back, not just in the arms. Reviewing various patent applications, I could see that the idea of fixing things on to the body was an area that had previously been explored by people interested in cameras. I saw designs where a pole was bent from behind the operator's back and dropped down like a fishing rod in front of the head, and the camera sat in that. The problem with all these designs is that they were fundamentally anchored to the body. Therefore the movement of the body was really going to affect how they worked: you were going to have to move in a very specific and rather stilted way. So that was a limitation.

I had also been visiting a store that sold push-bikes and things that go on bikes. The reason I went there is because these things are really evolved and beautifully designed with quick release. You get clamps that will fit very quickly to any piece of pole, and have adaptors on them. I used these adapted things to hold a microphone. And then, using Velcro, I'd stick other things on to them, and I could do these assemblies fairly securely and fairly quickly. Now, if you think of a pair of handlebars on a racing bike, which

40

work very well for stability – what if one could put a camera in the middle of a pair of handlebars? I took this idea and combined it with the idea of holding the camera in your arms, not touching any other part of the body other than your hands, but using your wrists, your elbows and your shoulders – thus giving you a combination of six joints, all of which are fluid and don't creak. And each of those joints absorbs vibrations.

So now we were looking for something where the weight of the camera, combined with the support system, was comfortable, not too heavy but heavy enough to give stability. We ended up with a rig which was basically a steering wheel with the camera right in the middle, using the circle of the steering wheel, which is tubular metal or carbon-fibre. The design works primarily in forcing the operator to take their hands off the camera. The hands are forced as wide as possible, with the camera put in the centre of a wheel so that the brain has more of a chance of judging what the horizontal stability line is. Then, on to this wheel – using push-bike technology – you can clamp a microphone holder, a light, or anything you want. For instance I discovered that Canon and Manfrotto made little controllers with a rocker switch that allowed you to control the zoom and the focus of the camera, and I could clamp one of those on too.

The biggest innovation in video camera design – which I think is a complete revolution – is the fact that the cameras now have their own screen. You no longer need to look through the viewfinder. My efforts to liberate the camera from the body – other than the hands – wouldn't have been possible if this innovation hadn't already liberated the camera from the eye. Previously your eye had to be glued to the viewfinder. Now the screen is something that you look at from maybe two feet away.

On a good film camera's viewfinder, you can judge your wobble while you are looking at the image. A video image is harder to judge. Also when you're peering through a viewfinder, your arms are bent, your shoulders are up, your head is jammed against the eyepiece – you're causing a certain kind of tension in order to hold your eye in one spot. Essentially you're scrunching all of your body movement into a tight position, and then locking it in there. The only movement you can make is from the waist, or with your legs. So when you see a handheld camera operator looking through an eyepiece, all of the elements of the body's design that could absorb vibration are locked, and therefore no longer functioning as a fluid joint. The opposite of that is to take the camera off the head, away from the eye. Your neck and your shoulders don't have to get tight. It's like the difference between good posture and bad posture.

4
Pre-Production, Part 1: The Budget

What Kind of a Filmmaker Are You?

I think it comes down to this. Many filmmakers, if they are honest, want to be photographed standing on a very large crane, next to a very large Arriflex, with about a hundred people in the background, all of whom are looking up to them with reverence because they are the Director. This is the quasi-Napoleonic notion of what a film director is.

Then there's another kind of film director. He or she would be more accurately described as an artist: a person who needs to work with other people in order to facilitate an individual idea – a more low-key idea – of what film is and how film can be made. And the present technology is very sympathetic to this second category, and somewhat annoying to the first category because this second option is now available.

Digital filmmaking requires an engagement of the sort that is best suited to an artistic viewpoint. But within that engagement there are very practical things that the artist then has to take on board – certain considerations and responsibilities that most artists would prefer to ignore. But this, I think, is what distinguishes film from painting.

Filmmaking is a communal activity in the sense that an artist has to go out and interact with a lot of other people and inspire and energise them. Unless you have the ability to convey your internal vision to enough people in a way that enthuses them and makes them want to help you translate that vision back as cinema vision, you won't make

43

the jump. And some people can't make that jump. But then some people could make the jump if they were encouraged to, and if they were told a few basic things.

Unless you involve yourself, you won't even have the possibility of making that jump – because there are, unfortunately, a series of mechanical issues that have to be dealt with, in the same way that you put an orchestra together. Unless someone books the orchestra, writes the parts out, books a rehearsal hall and makes sure there are sandwiches and tea in the interval, and pays them, you can be the greatest conductor in the world but the concert's not going to happen. And one could say that in conventional big-budget studio filmmaking, the orchestra analogy is very apt. Someone will make the tea, will book the hall, will pay everybody, and so on. If it's a good day and the wind's in the right direction, you can also step in and make everybody feel good and make the film work.

But below the protective barrier of money, in order to make a successful low-budget digital film you probably have to stand in yourself for the booker, the sandwich-maker, the paymaster and the others. Or you have to find a small group of your friends or colleagues to help you do all of those things economically. If these things aren't done efficiently, your result is going to be compromised.

Budget

Godard once said, 'Show me the budget and I'll show you the film.' That's the most useful piece of advice a film-maker can embrace. Because often the budget is something that people hide behind, on every level.

A filmmaker might have an ambition to shoot at a specific location on 35mm, and therefore, unarguably, the budget will inform you that you need something like £500,000, merely because the equipment and overheads – transportation, accommodation, etc – become totally inflexible, non-negotiable items.

On the other hand, I've been in situations where I've said to financiers: 'How much money do you think you can give me? I can make you a really erotic thriller, but just let me know how much I can have to spend.' And if they say a certain amount, you say, 'Okay, for that much I could shoot on 35mm for four days, or on Super-16 for ten days. If I went handheld, I could maybe get even more time. If I went on DV-Cam or mini-high-definition camera – if I don't carry too much equipment – that's maybe a month of shooting.'

It's a big mistake to overload the expectation of the film in advance by writing a script that is inflexible and highly ambitious, visually, in terms of location and look and equipment. That may well mean the film will never get made. On the other hand, if you concentrate on what is the *point* of the film – and if the script has a certain amount of tolerance built into it – you can then negotiate with yourself based on the reality that there is only so much money available.

I once tried to do a project called *How to Shoot a Movie*. It was going to be about a group of kids on a rough council estate who steal or somehow get access to film equipment from the BBC. One of them is actually a filmmaker, and in the opening scenes he goes to Foyle's bookshop and steals a book called *How to Shoot a Movie* . . . That project reflected advice I was given at the time: 'Black and white, and within an eight-mile radius of Bar Italia.' As a result of that advice my treatment was determined by the conditions that I never went too far away from London and used the minimum amount of equipment.

One of the failings of new film, I would say, is the inability to make a good marriage between the reality of the cheap, lightweight equipment, and budget. There seems to be almost a fear of stepping into a big, black unknown where you *can* make a film for nothing. Budget can no longer legitimately be used as an excuse *not* to make a film. Ten years ago you couldn't argue with that, because if you wanted the film to look halfway decent you would at least have to shoot on 16mm, and film stock and the rental of the cameras and equipment amounted to a certain financial wall which, unless you could get over it, meant that you weren't going to be able to make a film. But it is now possible to make a film for hardly any money at all. We see examples of it popping up at festivals – such as the film *Tarnation*, made using iMovie.

Even when I go to talk at film schools, I see a reluctance to go out and capitalise on what you can do with the equipment for nothing. You can make a feature-length film if you own or borrow a camera, and the stock for that camera is so cheap that for a couple of quid you get at least 16 minutes of high-quality tape. You can edit on any virtually laptop now. So often, though, people fall back on excuses to not make a film – possibly because filmmaking, suddenly being let loose and having complete freedom to create 90 minutes of visual storytelling, is still a very daunting idea.

I'll ask a filmmaker, 'How's your project going?' And they'll say, 'Well, you know, I'm still waiting to hear from so-and-so and so-and-so, and we haven't quite got the money together.' 'Really? What are you going to shoot on?' 'Oh, high-definition.' 'Oh, really? Wouldn't it be better just to shoot it on DV-Cam?' Which is very good quality, the equivalent of, say ten years ago, the best possible quality video you could hope to see in the world. But it's interesting that just as the quality seems to be getting better, people raise the bar of what they consider to be acceptable – often, I believe, as a reason or justification *not* to make the film. Because of fear.

Financing the Film

There are many ways to finance a film. The conventional way is to raise a lot of money, shoot on some form of film, probably 35mm, and with the kind of equipment that requires shooting over a period of five or six weeks. The minute you have committed yourself to spending that much money on the equipment and the format of the film, you are dealing with people who are giving a disproportionate amount of money to what, at this point, is an abstract idea – a script. You've crossed into a territory where you are inviting them to comment on the script, because it's their money. Therefore they feel they have a right to control elements of the film and that their taste should influence the story. Which is a disaster, because it's never been proved that the fact that you have money means that you have taste, or any concept of the way film works.

Usually people want to put money into film because they are attracted to the glamour of film, and they're gamblers. There's not a lot of difference between a studio and a group of bankers when it comes to putting money into a film. And these are the people you have tacitly invited to participate in the creative process. So when it comes to casting they will say, 'We think Gwyneth Paltrow and Brad Pitt should do this' – regardless of the psychology of the characters, because they are just looking at form. With casting you enter a very narrow world of possibility where there is a pool of maybe thirty actors based on their form at the box office, almost like racehorses – which is ridiculous because their form is measured on the success of the film they were in, not them.

My advice to all filmmakers is, at whatever cost, to try to avoid putting even one foot into that bath. Here are some examples of how one can do that.

If the film will be shot over a sufficiently short period, then you're not asking actors to jump out of the work pool for a significant amount of time, and you can work around their schedule. That way, you can get appropriate actors for the characters that have been written, some of whom may be unknown, and some – let us say – of a certain profile. But you should have the appropriate cast rather than the financially desirable cast.

Then you offer them each a minimum – what we call a 'favoured-nation' – deal, which literally means all actors get the same *pro rata* payment on a daily basis, and it will be a low figure. Actors do appreciate being offered good work, and they're not insulted by low payment – so long as they don't feel that somebody else is getting more than they're getting. So it's very important to have a level playing field, and for that to be transparent.

On top of this minimum payment, you offer them all some possibility of getting more money should the film ever become a success. This is what we call a deferred fee. You say, 'Okay, on paper I'm going to pay you £10,000. In reality, for the moment, I'm going to pay you £200. The balance – the £9,800 – will be given to you in increments once the film has crossed a certain break-even point.' In this way you could procure a famous actor and, on paper, pay them a reasonable amount of money – except that technically speaking you're not going to pay them that, at least not until you're in a position to, dependent on the success of the film – which itself may come about partly as a result of their name. The rest of your cast who are perhaps not so famous still get the same money as the famous actor upfront, but probably not as much at the 'back end'. There's a certain fairness to that, which is the proportion of your risk in relation to how famous your actors are.

Paying Technicians

Technicians are a different issue. Obviously, you *can* pay them at the low end of the scale, and you would then tend to look for younger technicians who are also working their way up the food chain in the film industry. But if you want a very specific job done – let's say, special effects or a certain kind of specialised photography – then within whatever your budget is, if it's *really* important, you will have to find the money to pay that person upfront. Technicians tend to not want a deferred fee. They wish to be paid as technicians because they're doing a technical job rather than a creative one, though those things do cross over.

That said, a lot of people have made very successful films by crewing up among friends who were at college with them, especially if they were at a film school. When I made *Hotel*, I put into practice an idea that had been building in me for many years. For some time I had been regularly receiving letters from people saying, 'I really like your work and I would love to work for you for *nothing*.' I started to keep them on file. And so with *Hotel*, people who had written to me or who I'd met or mentored through film school, I gave them all jobs – quite important, responsible jobs. I basically put them into the firing line, which was pretty frightening for them and, in some cases, worrying for me, because their lack of experience sometimes showed. For instance, I put four individuals in as the main camera assistants, and they were thrilled. But they forgot to do certain things such as cleaning the camera properly. So I had to bollock them severely, saying: 'You're not taking the responsibility seriously. If you were on a 35mm camera you would be fired for this lack of competence.'

There are many ways, if you have the ingenuity, to put a crew together and still stay under the danger-line of a budget which would take you into trouble in terms of the incremental loss of control that you would inevitably get – that every director gets, even famous directors – the minute you ask for more money. The question is simple: are you prepared to use your ingenuity, rather than just the muscle of the large budget?

One more thing about budget to always bear in mind is that if you sell yourself to the devil, one day he will come knocking on the door asking for repayment with interest. So the larger your budget, the less of the film you will actually own yourself. And should the film ever have success, it will be completely out of your hands. You will have sold that film to another party and you won't get a penny from it.

Of course, if you have sold the film to someone else then it is their responsibility to distribute the film, which they may do well or they may do badly. If you own the film then it's *your* responsibility to find a distributor. One of the main problems facing a digital filmmaker in the twenty-first century is distribution of your product.

But there's another factor to consider, which is that, as time passes in your career as a filmmaker, it will become more and more important for you to have a library of your work – as with, say, a novelist. You want to say, 'This is my book. It was published by this company, but it's my book.' It's always a mistake to give away all of your rights. In many instances that's happened to me, and I had no choice because these were large 35mm film projects. I watched with dismay as they were re-edited and badly released on DVD, and I had no control over them whatsoever. This is worth considering when you think about budget.

5
Pre-Production, Part 2: Location

'The Red Sea parts . . .'

For any feature film it's highly probable there's not going to be just one location – there are going to be many. The screenwriter tries to make the script as interesting as possible, and one of the ways of doing this is to keep changing the location, in the hope of stimulating the audience. And so we go from night to day, from sunshine to rain, and from domestic to exotic location. As someone once said, the opening description in *The Ten Commandments* – 'The Red Sea parts, the Hebrews surge forward' – takes about 30 seconds to write. But the filmmaker has to deal with trying to *realise* the words on camera.

When you sit down with a line producer, they start deconstructing your script into its nuts and bolts – number of extras, time of day, traffic control, weather control, flight path proximity, all these kinds of things. It becomes horrifying. You thought you'd written something fairly simple, now you realise it's extremely complicated. If you're making a feature, you don't want to confine yourself to such a ridiculous extent. To hamper your writing by the lack of possibilities in location because of the lowness of your budget would be too much of a restriction. Films have to have vision. So the trick is: how do you get the most out of your money in a location? And how can you bypass the need for excessive amounts of money to be spent in order to get some kind of vision on the screen?

Here as elsewhere, it will come down to your choice of equipment, the number of people on your crew, and the number of actors that you have to deal with.

Using a Location Manager

The location manager is someone who reads through the script, then goes off and takes loads of photographs and comes back to you with – let's say – for each location, ten possibilities. Each of these is usually in the form of a folder that opens up so that you see a kind of panoramic montage consisting of, say, ten photos, showing you what a particular street looks like. You then choose two locations that look particularly promising, and you get into a van and go look at those. It's always a strange moment when you arrive, because usually it will be nothing like as interesting as the street you had in mind when you wrote the script . . .

Once you've chosen the location, try to make a deal. On a conventional film, if it's a house you're after, the location manager would make a contract with whoever owns the house, or with the local police in order to have traffic control and so forth. This is all very complex and time-consuming and expensive, and I favour an alternative system altogether.

Wherever I go around London I'm constantly looking at streets and thinking, 'That's an interesting background . . .' And I'll immediately make a note of that as a location. I think it's an interesting skill or muscle to develop for filmmakers, particularly for writer-directors – to constantly look for locations which are quite simple. A restaurant, for example, where, if one wanted to shoot a scene with small video cameras, it's possible to go in and have a quick chat with the owner and say, 'Look, there's six of us, but we'll also come and have a meal here. Do you mind if we just shoot here for an hour?' Find out what night's not so busy for them and usually you can negotiate the desired result. So you get through the shoot of an entire film without ever resorting to the convention of a location manager and contracts and having to do deals with the police. You have to be careful, though, that you don't abuse the situation – because then you'll be shut down.

Manners

If you can go into a situation on the street with the minimum of fuss – a small camera, a couple of alert assistants, and actors who are able to be in a natural environment without being mollycoddled – you're going to have a far more convincing ambience on the film anyway, without becoming that upsetting or even that apparent.

Every time I've worked on a film – and this is something that increases with the size of the crew – the crew starts to behave badly in terms of its relationship to the location and the people who live there. And on large 35mm Hollywood shoots, I've always been appalled by the near-contempt that the crew often seem to have for the stretch of road or pavement they're working on, or for old people or disabled people . . . A common sight might be three bulky men, eating hamburgers, tool-belts dangling off their rather ample stomachs, completely blocking a pavement while people literally have to walk on the road to get round them. That immediately sets up a bad situation and causes resentment. Very quickly, people get bad-tempered and you start to encounter antagonism as people try to disrupt your filming.

Mainstream filmmaking advertises itself wherever it goes by parking twenty trucks and somehow staking claim to the territory, with officious PAs being rude to the public as they try to walk through – just because they're a film unit and they're setting up a kind of theatricality. Opposed to this is making a digital film, where you should sort of infiltrate yourself into a natural environment, and not try to change it. You don't stop the traffic, you don't highlight your presence, you don't put up a big neon sign announcing the film. It's rather like taking a stills photograph – in a subtle way, after a while people don't seem to see you any more, because you're not shouting, 'We need silence now!' Or, 'Stop the traffic!' And the director's not screaming, 'Who let that person through?' You just observe the environment sufficiently to know where to put the camera, and then you let the environment continue. The actors are then reacting to natural phenomena rather than fake phenomena. When you're shooting in a real location with a big film, one of the most ridiculous things I've ever seen is the traffic being stopped because the sound man will say, 'I need a pure dialogue track.' So they stop the traffic and it's very, very quiet, and then the sound man says, 'You're speaking too quietly, because we're going to have to add the traffic later on.' You then ask the actors to be completely unnatural by shouting in a quiet environment . . .

When I made *Leaving Las Vegas* – the first time I was in a position to control this – I told everyone we couldn't control the traffic because the authorities in Las Vegas didn't want us there. They didn't like the film. I said, 'It's fine, the actors will shout above the traffic.' The sound man and I discussed this, and one of the problems then would be that if we cut from one take to another within the master of the scene, it might well be that the traffic lights went red and the traffic went quiet for a moment. So in that instance we ran two tape recorders – one just on traffic noise, in sync with the second that was just on dialogue, which meant we always had natural traffic to mix in post-production. We didn't stop the traffic and I got, in my opinion, a much better performance from the actors because they were reacting to the traffic.

There's always some ingenious means for dealing with reality. One of the main structural points of new digital filmmaking is the way it has more of a relationship with documentary than with the conventional feature film, even though, at the end of the day, it's a drama. But audiences have become much more familiar – and, I think, much more comfortable – with naturalism in terms of the environment than with fake naturalism, as characterised by Hollywood filmmaking.

Moving from One Location to Another

You are constantly looking at the time-and-motion factor when you are making a film. How can you minimise the amount of time wasted on movement? It's very hard to move even as few as ten people smoothly. You get where you need to be and suddenly you're saying, 'Where's make-up?' or 'Where's Peter and Annie?' And you're told, 'Oh, we sent them off to get something . . .' But you can't start filming until they're here.

It's not often discussed but one of the things that's quite hard as a director is that you end up carrying a lot of equipment – lots of small things, all of which, at some point, are going to be essential. And you always want somewhere to put your things. If you're shooting in the street you don't really want to put your things down, because with the size of unit I'm talking about you don't really have enough people on your crew to have one person solely dedicated to making sure no one steals the stills camera . . . So you're constantly looking for one place to put everything in, so you can centralise the options. One of the things on a location that makes me completely paranoid when we arrive is the way people just dump things, apparently randomly, on the ground. You look around and there are bags everywhere. So much stuff is stolen from film crews because of the haphazard way that things are parked, because no one owns anything. I have more of a vested interest, because I see all my cases – three camera cases, a tripod case, a lens case, another case which has all of the accessories or the tapes – scattered across the floor.

This problem can be avoided by finding a base and staying there. So for each clump of locations you can say: 'Okay, here is a house we could have as our operating base for three days, and a hundred yards away from there is a car park, a hundred yards away is a tube station, and a hundred yards away in another direction is the lobby of a hotel that we can shoot in. Great. And let's have all our meals in the house.' And the minute that happens I feel, as a director, secure because I know I can put all my things in one room.

I adhere to a sort of military concept: when you arrive at your base, you consolidate everything very quickly. You put all the equipment together and you make sure someone's watching it. It's important. If someone steals a camera, you're prevented from carrying on, and it creates a bad atmosphere. So one of the first things I look for in a location is: where can we put things? One small room that we can lock – so immediately you have some kind of control of the technical stuff that you need to make the film.

The Relationship between a Film and Its Setting

Film is a form of storytelling. The human race is obsessed with storytelling because it expresses how we deal with the world. Everyone can relate to a good story. Within literature – one of the main areas which film comes out of – location exists in the mind. All it requires of the writer is to provide some descriptive passages – some writers write more, some less – which imply location, time of day, weather, season, etc, and then, having used a paragraph or two for that, they can get on with the story. In film, the use and development of location has somehow – largely through Hollywood – gone down a very specific path. Part of the experience of film is often the lush photography of a specific location. A James Bond film has maybe five, six, seven, eight exotic locations, and the opening and closing shots of those films are very important. Hollywood blockbusters spend millions and millions of dollars on locations or on fabricating the locations in the studio.

In the European tradition, certain locations exist in one's own environment and are very interesting – an industrial location, it might be, or if you live in Rome or a big city, the city itself is going to be the location. I elected to shoot *Hotel* in Venice because it was a location that I didn't have to build, and pretty much anywhere you point a camera is interesting. The colours already existed. I didn't need an art director to make anything look interesting: it already *was* interesting.

In my philosophy of film, the story is the most important thing and it shouldn't be so complicated to find an environment, or location, in which I can tell that story. If that philosophy appeals to you within the new digital ethos, then it won't be so hard to find a location, and then a couple of central bases in that location.

Let's say we've got a three-week shoot. It would be great if week one we had this base, week two we had that base, and week three we finally went to another one. So that almost as the script is being written you are envisaging that a large part of the action is going to take place in an apartment which has, say, an interesting view of a railway station. The railway station itself is an interesting location, and as long as my crew isn't too big I can probably steal quite a lot of the shots if I go in with just one camera and a couple of actors and we pre-plan what we're going to do before we got there. And let's say a hotel, which has a lobby and some bedrooms and a restaurant. That's another single location where we could, fairly economically and effectively, use one room as a base in which to put all the equipment and another room for make-up and hair, and we could probably use the bedroom as a specific location. So it's a very useful and productive creative process to be thinking of simplified locations when one writes. We have limited damage control already because there are always going to be huge problems when you start shooting, and you don't want to compound those by making the location itself a problem. Because once the location becomes a problem it will eat away at all your time and you won't be able to concentrate on your artistic problems, which may well be in the performance or in part of the script that doesn't work, and you need time to deal with those things.

Pre-Planning

The discipline of pre-planning is underestimated to almost tragic proportions. I've seen this with many student films, where they said, 'We're going to shoot in a disco', and I say, 'Really? That's great', and then I ask them about the inherent logistical problems and they go, 'Oh . . .' and look surprised. I have to tell them, 'Unless you deal with these now, you're going to have to deal with them when you get there, on the spot. It means you're going to be unhinged from your main purpose, which is to film a drama.'

One of the things I really enjoy is having a notebook with a page that's simply headed: 'Things that can and will go wrong on a shoot.' Every time I finish making a film, I make a little list of things that went wrong and I try to remember them for next time. The job of the filmmaker is to look at the script and say: 'Okay, in a perfect world this is what I would love to be in the film. Now if I imagine myself shooting this, what's the first thing that can go wrong? Is it the weather? Is it that suddenly a policeman will come along and say I can't shoot here? If that's the case, then I need to deal with that beforehand. Is it that there are too many people in a live location? That there may be people waving at the camera or literally getting in my way and I can't find anywhere to film?'

You have to spend enough time and really be honest about what could go wrong. And once you've got a list of what can go wrong you ask yourself: 'How can I deal with them now?' Probably you need to go back to the location and look again very carefully with all the potential problems in mind. Once you're forearmed in this way, you can designate a person to take care of them. But they have to be clearly briefed.

If your list is too daunting, it may well be that you have to blow a location out because there are too many possibilities of something stopping the filmmaking process, and you'll have lost time and money and momentum and energy. And that's a disaster. What I also tend to do is put a time limit on every location. So when the schedule is printed for the film, I almost insist on it being more specific than less. I say, 'We've got this scene to shoot in the lobby of a hotel. Let's say it involves five actors, not all at the same time, but they're all coming and going because it's the busy lobby of a hotel. I estimate that it's going to take three hours, so I'm going to allow four. And by halfway, two hours into this particular sequence, we need to have accomplished this. And if we haven't accomplished that, then we should realise that we're in trouble, we're behind.' Often it's not until the last hour of a four-hour scheduled shoot that people start to cop on to the fact that they're really behind.

Storyboards and Shot-Lists

If a scene is complex and it has some action in it, ultimately it's got to be a series of set-ups that the editor can get excited by. You need to go through the options with the storyboard artist – or yourself, if you're capable of visualising in that way. Then you can juxtapose one drawing against another and say, 'Oh, that looks nice, that's going to be exciting.' Don't rely on just trusting your instinct when you're actually shooting the scene. You might get a beautiful sequence but it might not cut together well because you forgot that the reverse angle is going to be crucial to the editor. So as part of the overall planning it's key that, even if you don't do storyboards, you at least do a shot-list. In the heat of the moment, if you haven't done such a list and you haven't ticked off the shots as you've done them, you'll be on your way home and you'll suddenly say, 'Oh my God, I didn't do a reverse . . .'

I always make a list in my notebook and tell myself, 'Okay, I need to do wide-shot coverage, medium-shot coverage, and then I need to give myself some cutaways and reverses.' Often, while I'm waiting for an actor, I'll see an interesting object and I'll just film it – it'll then be a point-of-view cutaway that may or not be useful to the editor. Always try to make the shopping list as sophisticated as possible.

The Function of the Director

The function of the director is to lead. And if you can't lead, then you need to appoint someone who can lead on your behalf, like a really good assistant director. Some directors are brilliant filmmakers but really don't have the desire to lead the troops. Somebody has to, though – because if no one is leading the troops, the troops will become lethargic and disheartened very quickly because they are working for you and they are trying to service your vision. Unless they have some energetic connection to your vision, they end up being functional technicians, and there is a cynicism attached to that. Either *you* have to do it, or you designate someone else to do it. I *like* doing it and, interestingly enough, the larger the crew and the larger the budget, the less generously received the leadership is. Very large film crews are very used to being autonomous within their own departments, and they don't like being helped. They don't like being told that they can do this quicker, and a sort of lethargy is built into the schedule in a way that I find exhausting and draining in terms of one's energy.

My favourite example is *Leaving Las Vegas*, which is the first film where I had enough control and where the schedule was unconventionally short for shooting a feature film at a lot of different locations on film, 16mm. So, in order to hit the targets, I looked at the budget and the schedule and the script and made sweeping decisions about equipment – handheld or on a tripod. Interestingly, the minute those rules were relaxed and the camera went on to a larger piece of equipment, or where the Director of Photography was allowed to light, we went over schedule and missed deadlines. I quickly dealt with those situations in a quite severe way. I said, 'That cannot happen again.' And each day I would say, 'Here are our targets for the day. We're going to this shopping mall and we have three hours to get the scene.

And that's non-negotiable. We will be out of there three hours later because our next appointment is an hour later in another location and that's also non-negotiable. So whether we have the shot or we don't have the shot, we will be leaving.' Inevitably, we got the shot – through a kind of practical reasoning of 'Okay, the only way to get this shot in three hours is to use this or that simple equipment.' And it looked fine. There's no compromise aesthetically in the film at any point. In fact the film looks better aesthetically through having had a Spartan approach to everything.

I've tried to carry on that philosophy in every film I've done since. The two times this really didn't succeed are the two times the budget went over a certain amount and we went on to 35mm. In both instances I was then unable to deal with or energise the crew in a way that I prefer. So, as a general concept, the director in the new digital filmmaking world has to be more responsible. If you are lethargic and sloppy, a lethargic, sloppy film will inevitably be the result. You won't get a sharp focus.

If you *can* lead, then in our new digital filmmaking situation the roles of director and first assistant director may be combined. You might not really have the money to have a first assistant, and often when you format the crew it's a good idea to look at the script and say, 'Do we really need this person?' It's also worth looking at the way theatre works: sometimes it's good to have someone making the film with you who functions almost like a dramaturge, like an intellectual parallel to you, because as a director you might get so sidetracked by the technical requirements of the shoot that you start to lose sight of the emotional and intellectual function of what you're doing. You become just a kind of technician because you are functioning a little bit as a first assistant director. You're in a four-hour shoot and after a certain time you look at your watch and see that you haven't accomplished what you'd set out to achieve by then, so now everyone needs to go quicker. You have to take that responsibility to hit targets on a regular basis, and once you start doing that, people start working at a higher energy. It's often forgotten that the function of a director is to create a collective energy within a location that is in direct relationship to the amount of time that you have been allowed to get the scene that you're setting out to do.

In summary, the responsibility of the director is to be hardnosed about the relationships between the script, the desired result of the film, the reality of the budget and the availability of the locations. You have to make difficult decisions based on the shared realities. The thing about filmmaking is that it is an accumulation of situations. By the time you get to the editing, you are dealing with the accumulation of all the choices that were made. It's a complex process.

6
Lighting

California *Über Alles*

The technique of lighting has evolved throughout the history of cinema. When the first cameras were constructed and the first emulsion stock developed, film speeds were *very* slow. This meant that in order to get a good exposure you had to use a lot of light – which is the reason why Hollywood was founded. The early filmmakers in America realised there really wasn't enough light on the East Coast to make movies, whereas California had sunshine almost 365 days a year. So an intelligent decision was made to go where the light was. The studios were built with back-lots where they did everything. The idea was to shoot in the open air with the sun shining – God's light.

Of course, at the same time people decided they wanted to shoot indoors as well. In order to do so, you had to approximate the power of sunlight, so hugely powerful bright lights were developed, with light bulbs that would give out a sufficient amount of light to allow a decent exposure within the camera – because you really had to thrust a lot of light on to the subject in order for the film stock to function efficiently. Those lights were very bright, very hot and *huge*. And the structures that housed the lights were even more huge. But thankfully, human beings are innovative, and so the camera and the lights began to develop in tandem.

The old system worked fairly efficiently for quite a long

time. As filmmakers themselves developed into specialists in certain genres – Westerns or epics or war movies that would, for the most part, use a lot of exterior locations – they wanted to have more control over the environment. A powerful film director might say, 'Yes, it's an exterior scene but actually I want to create it in a huge studio. I want to use a painted backdrop because I want complete control of the sound. We can afford it, so let's build it.' So you then start to see the development of interior artistic control by directors, in which lighting is, of course, still very important. That functioned very well and it also created a certain look, especially in black-and-white photography, where if you were using a very powerful light source to light your subject, it may have proved very uncomfortable and hot for the people on set but it looked very good on film. There's a dramatic, highly stylised look about black-and-white photography, and we love it. In a way, it became part of the language of cinema, and we're still a little addicted to it. But it's very much a 'lit' look, one where a huge amount of light is coming in left of the screen and creating shadows. It's essentially theatrical.

Then two things happened. One was that film stock got progressively faster and finer, which meant you no longer needed so much light. At the same time, manufacturers of cameras and lenses started to create faster lenses, requiring less light to get an exposure on to the stock, regardless of its speed. We have now reached a point where lenses have such low light possibility and their clarity is so amazing, and film stocks are so fast, that one could ask the question: why are we using artificial light at all?

I think the answer would be, 'Because that's the way

it's always been done.' . . . Also it affords a kind of control. Film technicians and filmmakers love the ability to control the light source; 'painting with light' has become the popular expression. But I find it quite bizarre that we really haven't moved on from the 1930s in terms of our attitude towards the camera and the lights, and shooting in a studio and having that artificial control of light. With digital technology you've now got these amazing cameras that are incredibly light-tolerant – lightweight, beautiful pictorial quality, depth of field, the whole thing – but they continue to light as if it was 35mm. Among certain professionals there is a stated assumption that in order for video to look good – and by 'good', they mean 'as close to film as possible'– you have to use a lot of light. I find this bizarre, because video is *not* film. And this addiction to a 1930s look is an anachronism which needs to be abandoned. Aesthetically, video functions at its most comfortable and most beautiful in much lower light situations. It has almost an internal glow. So it stands to reason that filmmakers should look at lighting in a different way.

The style of lighting that has been acceptable up until very recently – that sort of heightened golden light for everything, as epitomised by American television shows like *CSI* – seems almost dated now, in a sense that it's so far removed from how we now look at and think of reality. We've seen so many dreadful TV programmes – of the *Most Frightening Police Videos* variety – where the actual image quality is appalling and it looks like everything's been shot on VHS and yet the content, clearly, is exciting enough as these shows are very popular. One of the side effects of the plethora of these kinds of programme is that we've got very used to that look.

Recently I watched a BBC period drama shot on High Definition – set in a medieval Italian town, period costumes, hundreds of extras, clearly a very expensive production. To my way of thinking the mistake they made was to try to make video look like film, by using filters and a lot of light. The lighting was strange, because it lacked motivation: a lot of the scenes were set at night and yet there was too much light on the image.

Maybe it would have looked better if they'd shot it the way I shot *Hotel* – on DV–Cam – because at least it would have had a funky look to it. One of my main collaborators, Heathcote Williams, had done an adaptation of *The Duchess of Malfi* as a 'film-within-the-film'. So we were shooting sort of 'period punk'. It was like a fake Dogme period film. The actors wore period costumes and we used Venice as a period setting. The look of it was very successful. We shot one sequence, where the Duchess of Malfi is strangled in a Renaissance courtyard, lit purely with six blazing torches – that was the only lighting source. Now, it was perhaps a little under-lit, but it was enough. And with a little bit of help, if we'd used twelve instead of six torches, the light levels would have doubled and we'd have had a bit more depth of field. But it was the appropriate way to light something like that. There are all these myths about video needing more light. There are two schools: mine, which says you need less light; and then the school which says you need more light for video than you do for 35mm. Yes you do, to get a certain look, but that look is awful.

Colour

A digital camera is still a relatively new kind of beast for making cinema. As a filmmaker I think it's worth starting from scratch with the camera, spending some days just shooting images in different lights, with different variations on the controls. These can then be looked at or imported on to a computer very quickly. You can create your own colour scheme if you like, in the way that a painter would go and buy twenty tubes of oil paint and then get a palette and try different combinations of colours, making careful notes of the percentage of blue against yellow. Say, 'That's the green I really like, which is 40 per cent this and 60 that, and I might add a little bit of white as well . . .' So you create your own palette for your own eye. We all see things very differently. Some people like to see more blue, some like to see more red.

A series of articles in *American Cinematographer* addressed a very specific problem in digital filmmaking: how, in post-production, do you create a median, a law, of what colours are? How do you say 'This is a blue and this is a red', when everybody's mixing their colours on different palettes, on different monitors, different video equipment, and they're being projected by different manufacturers, and each manufacturer has a bias, maybe towards blue, maybe towards red? The issue is causing almost a panic among the film community. 'How do we get it all into one little tube?' The answer is: you can't. The genie definitely is out of the bottle and it's become a series of individual choices about a highly personalised way of looking at imagery and lighting. That's all the more reason why it's time to look at lighting in a different way.

On *Hotel* I had two approaches to colour. One was choosing to shoot in low light levels, and then adjusting the camera so that it compensated, at which point the colour really starts to pop in an interesting way. When shooting video, colour, if you under-light it, starts to glow as you push the grain on the camera. But if you over-light it, you'll flatten it and mute colour. The other approach was in post-production. There was quite a lot of saturation in the original *Hotel* footage, and then in post-production I started to take single stills from all of the major scenes because I was making a book about the film and I worked on those stills in Photoshop. I became very good in Photoshop at colour balancing, and I realised that there is a tendency in video for blacks to be quite milky. I discovered that by playing with the contrast, and increasing the black density of each image, as well as slightly pushing the saturation so that reds and greens and blues became more saturated – not to the point of distortion – then the film started to have a nice character, a density that I realised is often missing from video.

In the past there has been a kind of characteristic milkiness about video when it's transferred to film. I think that has been addressed by most contemporary cameras; for example, with the new innovative Sony High Definition mini camera – a very cheap camera – the image quality seems very rich and saturated, and the same with the Panasonic. But it doesn't hurt to look at each shot individually in post-production and try pushing them a little bit more, because there is something about film that is very dense and graphic. The reason why people often didn't like video was because they didn't feel they were getting that density. But if you take the Michael Mann film *Collateral*, which was shot on High Definition and film, you can see that it's now possible to combine 35mm, Super-16 *and* video without huge differences between one stock and the other.

Light and Shade

As filmmakers, for the most part, we're telling stories about people, so we're shooting individual human beings in an environment. It could be outside, it could be inside. It could be at night, it could be during the day. Could be winter, could be summer. What it boils down to is – is it very bright or is it very dark? If it's very, very bright, it's not going to look very good, so one would naturally attempt to somehow cut down the amount of light that's hitting the subject. Unless that's something that is written into the script – say, that the subject is blinking in bright sunlight and we have to have the feeling that it's so bright he or she can hardly open their eyes. Or it could be some kind of torture sequence in an interior, in which case it may be artistically essential to use a lot of light. But aesthetically, for the most part that's not going to look very good on film or on video.

So the first thing I do is try to take an actor out of the light, and into some kind of shade. Let's suppose that today it's sunny and then it turns overcast. When I come to cut my sequence together I don't want to have to be cutting from bright sunlight into shade and so on. So I'll choose some shade and I'll choose the background also to be in shade, so that the inconsistencies of the weather are not going to make the editing really complex later on.

Within the location that we have chosen, one of the considerations is going to be: what is the light going to be doing at two o'clock on Thursday? It might be rainy, it might be sunny. If it's raining, I don't really mind – so long as I've chosen somewhere where there's some shelter. But if it's sunny, I want to know that I have somewhere I can shoot in the shade as well, just so that I don't have an inconsistent look in my sequence when I'm finished. Exteriors are always a problem. The assumption that bright sunlight is the friend of the filmmaker is mistaken: sunshine is not anybody's friend, it's a nightmare. Nothing looks good in bright sunlight. If you were shooting a 35mm feature, you'd find it takes an agonising amount of time to put a huge white screen up, maybe 20 metres by 20 metres on poles with scaffolding, in order that the actor and actress can be in a sunny environment but without any direct sunlight on them because they're walking. That slows everything down to a crawl.

Interiors are obviously a different kettle of fish. Personally, I try to avoid using the conventional 'atmospheric' film lighting set-up – a key light on the actor, some rim light, etc. You see the same set-up applied to so many television dramas, and they look awful. But you will also see a better, more progressive TV drama where there are some practical source-lights in the room and then maybe one soft ambient light off-camera, just to give enough exposure so that little things are picked out in the room to give perspective. It's simply done. And with video you can get away with using soft practical lights more than in film. An angle-poise lamp pointed at a white wall is going to give enough soft light in the room, and it will be very flattering too, because it's coming from one side.

So as a digital filmmaker, just carry a couple of lights

with you. Look at the room you're shooting, then bounce some light off the ceiling or one of the walls. *Never* use direct light – not unless the script says that someone's being tortured with a bare bulb in their face . . .

There have been instances where I've really been pushed for time and I have reached for a couple of flashlights – the rechargeable kind that you put in the back of a jeep which have a hugely powerful tungsten halogen beam. If I have three of those, I can light any scene in any interior just by bouncing that light off a piece of white card or a white sheet or some silver foil – any number of surfaces that function as soft reflection. And to make a soft light just to fill in, I can just put a piece of Kleenex over the beam – or if I wanted it to be even softer, two pieces of Kleenex.

Wherever I'm shooting I always carry a soft bag containing a flashlight of the kind I've described and also a pocket-sized flashlight. If you screw the top off that light, the little tungsten halogen bulb is almost like a candle. And if you put a little piece of tissue round it, or if you've got some expensive film diffusion, just to take the nastiness off it, then you can hold that near someone's face but off-camera, and there'll be enough light to light their face.

Something else I use frequently are the very small flat-screen panels that are designed for viewing photographic transparencies. They're battery-operated, and I attach them as close to the camera as possible so they function as a soft portrait light.

Just think of the number of devices with lighting capacity that now exist. You can light a face by using a mobile phone. I've seen people in nightclubs with their faces illuminated by the display on their phone. I've found myself

75

scouting a location in a basement without light, and yet there's enough light from the mobile phone to see where you are. So many devices now have flatscreen monitors in them. There's literally enough light off the monitor of your video camera to light someone.

I also carry the flashing LED lights that you can clip on to the back of bicycles. Of course, they have a red cover on them, but if you take the red cover off there's just enough power in them to give the effect of, say, a neon light coming through a window. You gaffer-tape one on to a wall some-where and you get a little bouncing red light keying into the face. You could do a major lighting set-up from everything that's in my little soft bag without ever plugging anything into a wall. And when I do have the luxury of a wall socket, there are a variety of lights now on the market that use soft tubes lined up in a little case. You open the thing up and there are six thin tubes, giving off a very controllable, dimmable light – enough to light a scene.

One of the things I do with the actors is say: 'Look, within this room, these are the particular areas where the light is really good on you. Now, if you go out of that light you're going to become quite dark and indistinct – but, dramati-cally, you could use that to your effect. If you want to make an impact, come into a very strong light as you deliver a certain line, this is where the light is. So why don't *you* use the light?' I prefer this to the old technique of putting so much light in the room that wherever the actor stands they are lit – it just looks flat and boring. Or that agonisingly dull technique where actors have to learn to walk specifically from one spot to the next, because the DP or his focus puller has told them to. That makes actors into robots who just have to say their lines as soon as they hit their mark.

I've been in many situations where actors have done the most fantastic take emotionally and you say, 'That's great, I think we got it . . .', but then you look at the DP and he's making a cutting-his-throat gesture and mouthing, 'No, no, they were out of focus.' You say, 'Why didn't you follow them?' And the answer is that it's too complicated, because the camera department have set up such a complex camera movement that it's actually inhibiting the performance. What's liberating about digital filmmaking is that the cameras have such depth of field that you don't have to do that any more. Lighting is whatever you want it to be. Auto-focus on those cameras is pretty good. If you want to use it, it's accurate. If you don't want to use it, it can be tricky to override it. But camera manufacturers have caught on to the idea that camera operators like to be in control of their own focus, and so manual focus has become a much more user-friendly thing again. It's taken a long time for that particular penny to drop, but it has. For example, the Nikon stills camera has got the most amazing auto-focus, but I choose to use old lenses that are manual. No problem, you just press a button and you override.

Instead of expecting the world to be created for the film, it's now become much more a case of how you can fit into a world that already exists. You extend that to lighting. Every time I look at a light I ask myself: 'Would that be an interesting light to use in a film?' If it's a practical light – well, you're never spending more than £10 on a light fitting. The tube lighting that I just mentioned has become so popular its maker has brought out a mini version of it, a metre by half a metre. It's like a suitcase that you plug in and it's a beautiful light. I used one on a shoot and I said to the DP, 'Wow, that's really nice. How much is that?' He said, 'Oh, it's really cheap, about fourteen hundred pounds.' And I thought, 'It's just a light. I could buy a *camera* for that.' I might choose to rent that light, or if there was enough money in the production and the shoot was long enough, I might use the budget to buy one. But the difference between a £10 light and a £1400 light is not that great. It's like the joke about haircuts: 'What's the difference between a good haircut and a bad haircut? Two weeks.' It's almost the same with lighting. Within the kind of filmmaking that we're talking about, the benefits of the £1400 light don't justify its price.

The Camera's Own Effects

Lighting now functions with the camera in a very specific way. I've shot scenes completely in the dark using night-vision lighting, which was rather complicated, because you can't see what you're lighting unless you look through the camera. On a more practical level, with the Sony PD-100 I've slowed down the shutter speed and increased the gain on the camera to the point where I could shoot in a situation where it was so dark I could only make out the form of somebody by eye, but the camera could see them quite clearly, which results in a very stylised look – slightly blurred movement, because your shutter speed has gone down from, say, fifty to three frames a second, allowing it to expose. And if someone's moving you get what I call a Francis Bacon effect, which I find aesthetically interesting but it's been used wantonly on low-budget television and it's become a bit of a cliché.

That's an extreme. By fiddling with the camera you'll find the level of tolerance in terms of the low-light ability of the camera, where your additional lighting requirements are minimal. When you're shooting in a hotel or someone's apartment, just use the lights that exist in the room. Then really ask the question: in all honesty, is this acceptable? You will find it looks okay. You might say, 'Right, turn off the overhead light, let's just use the bedside lights. Ah, good, there's a bit of ambient light coming through the window.' But there's already enough light. Pretty much every scene in *Hotel* was shot using available light and existing domestic lights, or candles.

Low-lighting Van Morrison: Adapting to the Environment

In 2003 I made a documentary about the blues, and I persuaded Van Morrison to come along and be one of the musicians for a jam session. Of course, I really wanted to interview him for the documentary. I knew that I had a limited amount of time. Also, he's the type of person who, if he's not happy with a situation, will just walk out. So I said, 'Can I have half an hour for a quick chat with you?' And he said, 'Okay.' The artificial lighting in the Green Room was bad, fluorescent lights that gave it a horrible green flicker, but there was some light coming in from a window. I knew Van Morrison would be self-conscious if I added a light, or used a lot of technicians. So I had my camera, the microphone stuck on the rig that I'd designed – a perfectly adequate professional microphone. And the two of us were alone in this room, which wasn't very big. I made a decision very, very quickly to just shoot with the ambient light coming through the window.

The trouble was that the light was slightly over his shoulder. The great thing about a digital camera is you can look at the screen and see if you're getting a silhouette. So I then went into manual mode on the menu of the camera and changed the exposure until the window behind burned out and I started to get some exposure on his face. It was pretty grainy, but I felt, aesthetically, that it suited him. So then I could relax and just start filming and asking him questions. I knew I had a picture. I had headphones on so I knew I was getting sound. That's all I cared about really. And I got a really good interview out of him. I know I wouldn't have got a good interview if I'd brought in a light and said, 'Can you just give me ten minutes to do some lighting?' He would have become self-conscious. The fact is, we were virtually in the dark and he was very happy with that. If you can adapt to an environment – rather than getting the environment to adapt to you – you're going to get a better performance and a better result.

Experiments in the Field: *Timecode* and *Hotel*

I shot *Timecode* in Los Angeles in the late autumn of 1999, in daylight. Initially we shot in the morning, between the hours of 11 a.m. and 12.30 p.m. In the second week we added a second shoot each day, so we would break at 12.30 p.m. and shoot again at something like 3 p.m., so as to get in two complete takes. And that became interesting, because around 4.30 p.m. the exterior light started to get more reddish.

The main adjustments for interior shooting were based on the idea that because each camera was shooting a 95-

minute take, and most cameras at some point would be outside and inside, you'd have to balance exterior sunlight and then go inside. In one instance, we go into a very dark cinema. It was literally a blackout. So we rigged very small lights to give just the minimum amount of light and told the actors to be aware of those lights. In the main conference room – where all the executives were sitting and where the shooting takes place at the end – we had some soft lights in the ceiling to give a general light there, and we used neutral density filters on the windows in some instances to be able to pan from an interior shot to something that was happening outside on the street, like when Stellan Skarsgård is coming to work. In that instance, I was shooting it and I used a very small square of strong neutral density filter, which is basically a filter that just cuts out light; it doesn't change colour. I would pan to the window and, because my exposure was set for the interior, in general the exterior window would just burn out, except for this one patch where the neutral density filter was, which would be balanced the same as the inside of the room. If I zoomed into that, I could clearly see outside without changing my aperture. We cameramen had to do our own focus and also constantly change our aperture setting based on the room that we were in at any given time and whether we were interior or exterior. But that could be done by eye, just by looking at your monitor. If it's too dark, you slowly adjust.

As time wore on, we all got very good at doing it quickly; we'd know instinctively how much to open up the lens. And because we couldn't stop and take the camera off our shoulders, this all had to be done while you were shooting, so we had to find ways of making a transition so the audience wouldn't notice.

Hotel was shot in a series of much shorter takes than *Timecode* – in that sense, more conventionally. So we were able to look at each set-up and at the lighting that existed in that space, try it out, and if it needed help then, in those extreme circumstances, I would say, 'Okay, we can add a little bit of light somewhere. But if possible, let's just use a domestic light to do that, an anglepoise lamp or something.' One of my favourite lighting sequences is the scene where the maid comes into Rhys Ifans's room and does a monologue about her parents. It starts off with her at the door, pretty much in shadow. There's a light outside, so when she opens the door you're aware of the fact that there's light in the corridor behind her. She closes the door and she's standing in shadow but you can still see her face, and the camera is shooting across Rhys Ifans, who is bathed in very strong light from an anglepoise lamp next to the bed. And she very slowly walks and talks and comes up to him. Then, at a certain point, she hits the kind of periphery of that anglepoise light and her face starts to get brighter until finally she brings her face very close to his. This is about a ten-minute sequence of dialogue in one take. And she's now in the same light as him so they're balanced.

There are two elements of that sequence that I was especially proud of. One was that the camera was handheld on the fig-rig with no support other than the rig, just resting on a table. I was operating it sitting in a chair, my elbows locked, with just my hand very lightly on the zoom control button so I was able to smoothly go in and out of the shot.

It looks like it was shot on a tripod. And, secondly, that one light source was not only adequate but the appropriate light for the entire sequence. I've seen it blown up to 35mm and on a huge screen and it looks amazing. Just a standard light bulb in an anglepoise lamp . . .

Laying Off the Masters of Light

Right now the Director of Photography is a breed in danger of extinction. There was a time when the DP had to be able to know exactly what the image was going to look like when it came back from the lab the next day – his or her experience with the film stocks and the processing allowed a 'virtual' understanding of what the results would be. This is no longer a valid skill. If you shoot on film, the monitors will give a reasonably accurate idea of the image rendition; and if you shoot on video then you get instant gratification. So this quasi-mystical figure of the DP has gone, consigned to history.

Do you need a DP at all? Well, yes, of course you do. Someone has to shoot the film and take the responsibility for the image. But it's worth re-examining the job description in the light of the new camera technology. Studios use computer geeks to 'animate' sequences before they're shot, and sometimes DPs are presented with those animated sequences and told that this is how the scene should be shot. Film stocks are fast vanishing, and the future is digital. I believe that film will survive, albeit in a much reduced form, but what is vital for the survival of the art of filmmaking is that we quickly re-examine the role of the DP. This person still has to understand the principles of lighting and camera movement. But now would be a good time to ask some basic questions like, '*Why* this lighting?' and '*Why* this movement?' In a way, this going back to basics is like reinventing the cinema.

7
Camera Movement

Perpetual Motion

In the early days of cinema cameras were necessarily very heavy and, because of their value, considered very vulnerable. So the best thing one could do with them was to secure them very tightly on a tripod or similar support, then turn them on and leave them alone, with the actors moving in and out of a fixed frame. It was a successful system, but very much a deference to the world of theatre, with the camera basically filming a sort of reversed proscenium arch – actors knew where the edge of frame was, close-ups were when the actors walked towards the camera, a wide shot would be when they walked away, and so on. The camera lens approximated the eye of a viewer sitting in the ideal position amid the audience.

But very quickly, as the excitement of cinema took hold and filmmakers began to get more innovative and competitive, the camera started to move more, and that was an exciting development. The viewer suddenly moved to a new reality, away from the idea of being a fixed head watching a play and towards the notion that one somehow *was* the camera and therefore a participant in the drama. We could say that this was the real birth of cinema.

As editing and the various ideas of montage developed – jumping into a close-up, then jumping to a reverse angle – the immediacy of the way these devices took you into a story must have been totally captivating for early audiences. This way of telling a story on a huge screen is sensual beyond belief. Then the talkies came in and brought big sound. It was *the* twentieth century innovation in storytelling. But, human beings being what they are, we get addicted to something very quickly, and as our tolerance level rises we need increased stimulation. In a way, the history of cinema then became an issue of: how do you deal with the problem of visual stimulation? You're delivering large quantities of sensual reality, adrenaline-inducing phenomena, an experience very different from reading a novel or sitting in a theatre. Camera movement thus became one of the major devices with which to activate an audience and maintain their interest.

Unfortunately, there's a breed of young filmmakers who have grown up getting terribly excited by the long opening take in *Touch of Evil* (1958) and the long Steadicam shot through the nightclub in *GoodFellas* (1990). They are geeks. They think they know about camera moves and they're in love with camera movement, but they have no understanding of camera movement psychology. For them, of course, if they just planted a camera, blocked it off, and had interesting action taking place in front of it, their job would be redundant. So what's happened is that these people in love with camera movement – which they think is somehow 'pure cinema' – have turned into self-proclaimed 'visualisers' and have claimed a position of power within the system. In fact they are the perpetrators of bad camera movement, and it's like a virus that's gone through cinema.

Should You Move the Camera?

If you want to move the camera you have to have a very good reason why. Hitchcock, for instance, might say: 'Because I want to scare the audience. So my idea is to have the camera creep up behind someone like a stalker.' Good idea. Well, we can invest in that, so let's get some track and a dolly.

Or suppose we want to begin a film like the opening chapter in an epic novel, where they describe a valley and a little house, and as we get closer to that house and enter inside it we see Mr and Mrs Smith. Good idea, but we might need a crane to make that really play. So the crane became the means of doing something akin to 'chapter headings' in film. We sweep in. It's beautiful. And seeing such grand camera movement, an Eastern European composer might say: 'I'll write something epic for that, it's crying out for sweeping-crane-movement music!' So, through this desire to stimulate the audience, you began to see very quick and parallel developments of technique – how to move the camera, how to make a big noise, how to steal the score from contemporary classical music.

But just as people get addicted to heroin or cocaine or alcohol, the movie industry became addicted to these big movements. In truth, if you took them away, you'd still have the ability to tell an amazing story, so long as you had actors and the benefit of human experience. Of course, fine films were still being made without recourse to these sweeping bravura techniques. My quarrel with camera movement is at the point where the intelligence that had gone into deciding why the camera should move changes to the demand that the camera *has* to move, because if it doesn't then there's the possibility that the audience might get bored. Camera movement has become, in a way, the slave of the system, to the extent now that most of the time when I watch a film it seems to me the camera movement has no dramatic justification whatsoever. In the same way, baroque music quickly degenerated into a series of affectations and ornamentations of notes. You couldn't just play the note G – it had to be framed by a G sharp and an F sharp, with a trill . . .

For me, the function of camera movement is to assist the storytelling. That's all it is. It cannot be there just to demonstrate itself.

Needing to Move the Camera

Imagine you're watching a film in which there's a dinner-party scene. You might well find that the camera has been put on a track, and it's moving very slowly around the table, all the time, and there's foreground and background movement that the editor can successfully cut together. I would ask the question: who is the camera at this point? And why is it moving? There's probably no real answer, other than that we're addicted to camera movement.

Now imagine shooting that dinner party with the camera locked off in a series of positions, with which the editor will be comfortable when cutting the scene together. Assume that at a certain point, there's a sudden revelation from one of the guests. At that point I'd want to add movement. But I probably wouldn't want to actually move the camera – I'd probably want to just creep in on a zoom, very slowly – so slowly that the audience isn't aware of it, just enough that the movement registers psychologically, even subconsciously, in such a way as to heighten the moment of revelation. And if, by the end of the scene, the camera would have moved from a medium close-up to a close-up without the audience being aware of it, then I would consider that to be a successful camera movement – one that had not in any way called attention to itself. Whereas if you've already done a lot of endless sloppy slow tracks around the guests, then by the time the move comes in on the revelation the coin has been devalued to such an extent that it no longer has the value it needs.

In 2004 I broke my leg and I had to take painkillers. I took ten a day. And I told my doctor they really weren't effective and I wanted something stronger. He said, 'Well, there isn't anything stronger than the ones you're on.' At a certain point I realised that I was losing the ability to think straight, and I stopped taking the painkillers. Four days later, I took one painkiller and it had such a powerful effect on me that it stopped the pain and also stopped me in my tracks, because I was so aware of the radical effect of the painkiller. My point is, try to preserve the effect – don't dilute it by overuse. It's not that we've crossed a line and the technique no longer works. It just needs a slightly more barren environment in which to thrive – so that when you intelligently decide that you *need* to move the camera, it will be effective.

My rule about camera movement is simple. Always ask the question: why is the camera moving? And if your answer is, 'I don't know', then put it on a tripod. Just find the best place for it. Where is the best place? There is no rule. It's a question of how good your eye is. I find that when I'm operating a second camera to the DP's first camera, he chooses the best place to put the camera. In my opinion, I then find a better place once he's set up, because I don't have the responsibility of carrying the scene any more. But I find a really interesting angle. And in the same way that I'm always looking for locations, I'm always looking for angles. So you half-close your eyes, you look at something, and you move around the room until the relationship between the person and the room and the objects is at its most interesting.

Putting Yourself in the Firing Line

Sometimes it's necessary to imprison the actor in a very tight environment where there's a specific limit to what they can do. That limitation will be for a specific psychological reason. Other times, I will let the actors go where they want. In that instance, the camera is handheld so that I can follow them and create a dynamic between them and myself, the camera, which will empower them in some way.

When it comes to highly personalised filmmaking I favour the practice of putting yourself in the firing line with the actors, as opposed to the conventional approach whereby the camera is put in a safe place and the actors play to it. If one is directing a scene in an apartment, between, say, a husband and wife, or any two people – a John Cassavetes sort of scene – and some tension is developing, then the psychology of the camera and the attitude of the operator to the actors becomes crucial. You have to put yourself in the scene as the camera. It's a hard thing to explain. It's the difference between trying to pretend you're not there – which is really not going to work in this environment – and crossing a line to say, 'I am the camera and I'm part of the scene now.' I've operated on scenes using a video camera on a very wide lens, where the camera has ended up nine inches from the actor's face because I've pushed the camera into a close-up rather than zooming. The minute a camera gets that close to an actor, they will start to respond in a good way. Actors like having the camera close. They feel they're really in the scene – particularly, if the camera is so tight to their movement that whatever they do, they feel the camera's going to go with them – it's not detached, not impersonal, not floating over their shoulder . . .

In my more recent films – particularly *Timecode* where everything was in one take and therefore everything had to be on camera because there was no chance of cutting away later on – a key element for me has been the physical proximity of the camera to the actors. The involvement of the camera person within the scene has been deliberate and important. It's been a conscious decision of mine – that filmmakers be far more involved in the film than before.

Close-Ups

One of the characteristics of digital cameras that I particularly like is that they have such deep focus. With most film cameras the depth of field is limited, and so focus becomes crucial in respect of the actor's movement, since it's so important that the character is always in focus. Most digital cameras, though – certainly when they're on their wide-angle mode – have such depth of field that you don't really have to worry about focus. They're auto-focus anyway. But one of the things you have to try to do is filter some of the light out of a video camera because sometimes it's so in-focus that you see every speck of dirt on the lens. One of the things I quite like about this is that it sometimes forces the camera person – if they're working on wide angle and they want to go into a close-up – to actually move into that close-up physically.

Cartier-Bresson would say that if you want a close-up of someone then you have to get close to that person to take it. You can't steal the shot with a long lens or a zoom lens. And if they object to you being that close and they want to punch you in the nose, then you have to take that on board. Borrowing that philosophy, I'd say: Leave the camera on a wide shot and then if you want to get some impact, move very carefully and delicately into a close-up. Or move in quickly if you want some impact. But don't hide behind the technical capability of your camera by zooming in. Create the frame by your proximity to the person – and that will enhance the psychology of the scene. If they see the camera literally moving in tight, the actor will increase the tension of the scene themselves. To me, that was the real revelation with these cameras, and I liked it.

The Close-up in Wide Angle

There are two films in particular that I would cite as classic examples of the art of wide-angle cinematography. One of them is *Knife in the Water*, Roman Polanski's first feature. It involves three people on a boat – a very small boat, where obviously there wasn't room for a lot of crew or equipment. The only way Polanski could shoot was on an extreme wide-angle. So he stylistically adapted to that reality by using the distorting quality of the wide-angle lens in close-up. And because the style comes out of a completely practical, almost non-negotiable need to use that lens in that environment, it works on every level. The other thing to bear in mind is that if you've got a very wide lens, your camera movement is going to be far more fluid and steady than if you're on a telephoto lens. Just the nature of the wide angle means that it creates fluidity in its movement.

The second classic wide-angle film for me is *The Hill* with Sean Connery, directed by Sidney Lumet, which takes place in a prison. Ossie Morris, the DP on the film, was faced with a set of interiors that were very claustrophobic, and with five characters in there. His choice was between shooting them as an endless sequence of close-ups and having the editor cut them together, or choreographing the scene with a wide-angle handheld lens, so that actors coming in and out of the shot had a slightly distorted and surreal quality to them. In all of the interiors – the narrow corridors and the interior of the cells – a handheld wide-angle camera is employed. And sometimes the actor Harry Andrews, who plays a sadistic sergeant major, comes so close to the lens that his face distorts. If they're photographed closely with a wide-angle lens, figures of authority become very menacing.

8
Working with Actors

'Are you nervous?'

An actor can be (a), a highly trained individual who has studied the art of acting in some kind of educational establishment, and then, through fairly regular experience in film and theatre, has developed all of the skills of acting; or (b), someone who is untrained and has little technique but perhaps has a good instinct for performance.

The way that you would relate to these two types of actor would be different. Sometimes it's a situation where you need to help with the technical process of acting, in which case you need to know a little bit about acting technique yourself. On the other hand you may have to deal with some kind of emotional blockage. This is not a technical issue, it's psychological, so you need to understand a bit about the emotional states that come with the job.

An actor is someone who is, apparently, able to impersonate or embody the personality and character of another. In crude terms, they're able to make us believe that they're someone they're not. In order to understand acting, try to be an actor for an hour in front of a group of people; in other words, stand up and take any scene that involves some sort of emotion or characteristics that are not currently your own – with text that has been written down or you're going to improvise – and see what happens. For the most part, for people who are not used to acting, it's an agonising experience. It's embarrassing, it's awkward, it's perverse. It's extremely difficult to find within yourself whatever is required from the text or whatever it is you're trying to deal with. At that point you'll realise that acting is an incredibly difficult thing to do.

One of the problems that we have with actors is that, for the most part, they're good at it. Therefore we make the assumption that it's easy for them. In 1989 when I made my first feature film in America, *Internal Affairs*, I played a cameo role, because I had myself been an actor of some description – it was within the area of performance art, but I was used to the idea of playing a character on stage in front of large numbers of people whom I didn't know personally. Because I was comfortable and familiar with the idea of acting – and also for a bit of a laugh, and because we all know that certain directors did cameos in their films, notably Hitchcock – I was persuaded by the casting directors to do a cameo in *Internal Affairs*. I played a rich man called Mr Hollander who ran an art gallery and I had three or four scenes, including one with Andy Garcia, who was a very volatile actor. In fact, I ended up being knocked out by him because the stuntman was in the wrong place.

I had been busily directing when suddenly I was told by the first Assistant Director that I had to get into costume quickly because one of my acting scenes was coming up quite soon. I had totally forgotten that I had elected to be in the film so soon. So I got changed very quickly. Just before I did the scene Andy Garcia came up to me and said, 'Are you nervous?' And I said, 'Yeah, I'm really nervous.' And he said, 'Good. Every time you shoot a scene you should remember that. The actor is always nervous, regardless of who that actor is.' And I have remembered that – it's stayed with me and I know that it's true, however confident actors seem to be. The apparent confidence actors sometimes have can be a real barrier to directors who don't know anything about acting, because they themselves are nervous.

Being Intimidated by Actors

Young directors tend to be frightened of actors. It's hard to fathom how actors do it. If you put yourself in their situation, you know you couldn't do it.

On the first day's shooting of my first proper film, *The House*, the producer had for some reason scheduled the most complicated dialogue sequence in the entire film. It involved nine actors in a room, all talking, in period costume, with a snowstorm going on outside. And they were heavyweight actors – Nigel Hawthorne, Stephen Rea, Alun Armstrong – I'd never worked with actors of this calibre before. But the scene was set up and it looked fine, and then the first Assistant Director turned to me and said, 'So what do you want to do first?' And I had a complete meltdown. My brain froze. Just a white-out. I didn't know what he meant. 'What do you wanna do?' Everybody just stared at me. I just didn't know what I was supposed to answer. All I knew was I wanted to make a film.

Thankfully Nigel Hawthorne took pity on me and said, 'Dear boy, I'm assuming that we'd start with a wide shot. I've got the first line of dialogue. What do you think if I walk over to the fireplace and I turn and then warm my bum on the fire? Because the next line's with Stephen. I was assuming that you'd probably want to cover that in close-up later on . . . ?' And he talked for long enough for me to get my brain back, until I said, 'Yes, I think that's going to work very well . . .' So we did the first shot, and I never looked back. But that first shot was a complete nightmare. I just didn't know what to do. I was intimidated by these actors. I'd met them all in casting, they were delightful, I had such respect for them – they were all older than me, for the most part. But suddenly faced with telling them what to do, I didn't feel competent. I didn't feel qualified. But they just want to know what it is you want. Then they can tell you how they can do it, and give you choices. But they can't give you that answer until you tell them what it is you want from them.

Some actors that I've worked with are very intimidating and unkind towards inexperienced directors. But 99 per cent of my experience has been that actors, if you treat them with respect and ask for their expertise, will share that expertise with you. They'll be delighted to show you what their choices are. In fact, in some instances, the more inexperienced you are, the more comfortable your relationship is going to be. It's only when you start to think you know what you're doing with actors that you come up against some resistance – because they've turned up on set with a very clear idea of what they think the scene requires in terms of their performance. And they deliver that and you say: 'Well, it's not exactly . . . How about trying it this way?' And then you may have to spend some time with your ego and theirs, and yours has to win because it's your vision and it's your film. You can't just say to someone, 'No, that's rubbish. Do it this way.' You have to say, 'That's very interesting . . .' It may well be that you see something that you never imagined in the scene – that's the joy of working with a great actor. You may end up with a performance that bears no resemblance to the one that was in your head. It's better, because the actor is really good at their job. But if you don't give yourself the possibility of that happening then you've also wasted an opportunity with a really talented person.

A few years ago I directed an episode of *The Sopranos*. I was a fan of the show and thought the standard of writing and acting very high. I didn't get to meet the actors until the day before the shoot – they were still shooting the episode prior to mine. But we all met for an hour and there was a reading of the script. I realised that I was the only person in the room who really had no clue what was going on – a strange feeling for a director. The actors were friendly but cool, and I felt very much the outsider.

We began work early the next morning on a fixed set – one that gets used in every episode of the show – so there was the minimum of lighting to do. In a frighteningly short amount of time I was given the set and the actors. The scene involved Tony Soprano (James Gandolfini) and his gang of guys, and was essentially a piece of double talk, in that information was given to Tony that he already knew but didn't want to reveal to his guys because . . . well, it was complicated stuff. So I was given the floor, and I suggested a camera set-up that I felt would convey the subtlety needed. I described it in my very English voice, and then James Gandolfini stared blankly at me and said something like, 'Why the fuck would I do that? Tony Soprano wouldn't do that.' It got very quiet, and suddenly I had everybody's attention. I tried to keep my cool but I felt very intimidated by these actors and the crew. So I suggested that he first try the way *he* thought would work, and for several minutes the actors did just that. I sat and watched while nothing worked. Then Gandolfini said, 'Okay, let me try something else.' He stopped and thought for a moment and then did exactly what I'd asked him to do in the first place. It worked fine. He had his back to me and then he turned, a huge smile on his face, and said, 'Hey, did I tell you what a thrill it is to work with you? I love your films, this is going to be fun.' Steve Buscemi told me subsequently that Gandolfini liked to test directors this way. Scary stuff, but you have to hold your ground somehow.

What Happens When a Scene Doesn't Work

You're a fledgling director, you have your actors, there is a text, the actor or actress comes on and they do the scene and it's not working for you. Now the fact is, there are virtually no laws or no reason why the scene *should* work just because someone's written it. Often the writer hasn't taken into account factors which have suddenly become apparent when the actors try to do the scene. This could be a huge cause for despair. On the other hand, if one works on the basis that the script is a good starting point for actors to start saying the lines and interacting – then the real work now begins.

If the scene doesn't work and you're also dealing with a hundred different things, such as the lights or the weather, often the director will behave badly to the actors by saying 'Come on, let's do it again' – and if the actors say, 'Well, what do you want differently?' the classic response will be,

'I'd like you to do it better.' Which is a pretty stupid thing to say to an actor, or to anybody. Of course the actor wants it to be better, but specifically how? The problem is that often the director really doesn't know what will make it better. They only know that it doesn't work. So immediately there is some tension because the actors feel they're not giving their director what they want, that they're somehow failing. They become nervous and aggressive, and the director in turn becomes more nervous and aggressive – or despondent – and the scene can quickly go from bad to worse.

By the time you're into your fifth take and it's still not working, you've run out of vocabulary. The actors will start saying, 'I don't know what you want. Tell me what to do different.' And your brain starts to freeze. Everyone is now staring at you – you are the director and you don't seem to know what you're doing. You don't seem to have an answer, and as your nervousness increases so does your insecurity. Theirs increases too, but it sometimes takes the form of arrogance because they're actors and they can impersonate confidence. They won't look like you. You'll look like the nervous one. You've made them feel inadequate because they can't seem to give you what you want. Now they start to think that the script is crap and they talk among themselves and say, 'This is just a fucking load of rubbish. First-time director, of course, what do you expect?' And very quickly you've created two camps. The minute that happens, it's a disaster. Your job as a director is to spot the camps as they start to establish themselves, and then nip the problem in the bud straight away and say, 'You can't have a separate camp. Everyone's in the same camp here and we all have to talk to each other.'

Part of the art of leading is to admit that you're sometimes wrong. I've been in situations where I've done a
rehearsal for a scene and I've just said, 'It's crap. The scene
isn't working. Let's just take twenty minutes out. I just want
to think about this.' Sometimes you just have to buy time.
And that's a scary thing because it seems like everyone's
looking at their watch and saying, 'We've gotta be out of
here.' If it's a really serious situation, you need to calmly
buy as much time as possible to think – with someone else
usually, someone whose judgement you value, whom you
can ask, 'What do *you* think? You were watching.' And often
they'll say, 'Maybe you're just being a little bit hard because
it didn't seem that bad to me.'

When I was making *One Night Stand* I had a confronta-
tion with Wesley Snipes. He questioned the substance of
a scene, and said that he found it hard to believe that he
would do what was in the script. It was a scene where he
spills ink on his shirt and Nastassja Kinski offers him her
room in which to change. Wesley – quite correctly – said
that he wouldn't go upstairs with a strange blonde
woman to change a shirt. His body was in great shape,
and he'd change right there in the lobby. 'So why am I
going upstairs with her?' Again, this was a very public
debate in front of the crew and the actors. I thought for a
while and said the following. 'Wesley, you are entirely
correct, the scene is not particularly well conceived and, I
hope, will occupy only a short amount of time in the film,
so that the audience doesn't come to the same conclusion as you. However, without the scene the film will not
work – there will be no romance. So I rely on your amazing ability as an actor to get us through this moment con-

vincingly and quickly.' He was happy with this response and did just that. The mistake would have been to argue the point.

As a director your judgement is being kicked left, right, front, back all the time, because once you start making the film all you're doing is answering questions. I don't care if it's a major feature film or a digital film, you're still answering questions. 'What do you want?' 'What do you want next?' 'What will you want tomorrow?' 'What time do you want lunch?' 'Are you going to have lunch?' 'Do you think we'll go over?'

A particular favourite goes like this:

'The actor is upset. She's in the trailer and she's been crying. I think you should go and talk to her.'

'Why?'

'Because she thinks you hate her.'

'I don't hate her.'

'Yeah, but just now when they didn't do the scene very well, you said such-and-such and you didn't notice she was crying when she left. She's not going to come out of her trailer until you go and talk to her.'

You should be prepared for the fact that all those things are going to happen. It's almost a government health warning, but the film *Living in Oblivion* – a film about making a film – illustrates all the things that can go wrong on a low-budget shoot.

Partly because I have been an actor and am used to the idea of improvisation, and partly through experience, my resolution to an impasse is to sit down and say, 'Let's talk about this, okay?' I've been in this situation with very famous actors on very expensive films. The end scene had been written and it really didn't work. And the things that go through your mind if you stay calm – which you have to – are:

Firstly: 'What is the point of the scene? What do we hope to achieve by the end of this scene?' That's the most important thing.

Secondly: 'What material do we have and why isn't it working?' That really can be ascertained quite quickly and calmly.

And thirdly: 'What do we do about it? What can we do to achieve the goal? By the end of this scene I want this information and I want to know that the characters are now in a new position. Because the next scene won't work unless this scene works – that being the nature of film.'

Usually at that point, if you have engaged the actors in that process of creativity – which they're very good at – they will have suggestions, some of which won't work but some that will. And the job of the director is not to let it get out of hand, and basically say to the actors, 'Okay, let's just improvise it. Over to you . . .' Allow them to participate but at the same time maintain some kind of overview – because *you* know the whole film. Sometimes you've got to say, in the most diplomatic way, 'That's a good idea but the problem with that is if we do that, it's going to create an imbalance later on.' So you need to always hold it down with something. If you constantly explain what the context of the particular drama is, then the actors can often be very helpful and creative. Certainly, quite quickly there is enough confidence and openness on the set that it becomes enjoyable. And the minute the tension dissipates a little bit, the creative potential goes right up.

The lesson is this: actors do not have your overview – let them in!

The joy of making a digital film is that you have more time with the actors because you're not spending five hours with the lighting. 'We are here to work and solve this problem. We have got three hours. It's a five-minute scene. Okay, let's just try it. Let's just run it as written, but now let's calm down a little bit, take a few more pauses.' And so we run it again and the actors try something. And within that second try you immediately spot something and you say, 'Ah, that's interesting . . .' And as soon as you finish the take, you go straight over to the actors and say, 'I've seen something, it's really starting to work. It hasn't solved the problem of the scene yet, but I think it could be the key to taking us in a new direction. So why don't you adjust that? And let's run it again as quickly as possible.' Now the actors are working, which is what actors like better than anything. Actors really like acting. It's not often acknowledged. People often think they like sitting in trailers. They hate that. What they love is the moment of interaction with another actor and a camera. So what you want to do is give them as many opportunities as possible to do that.

So you run it again, and they run a little bit with this new idea. And you say, 'Yes, that's now highlighted something else.' But, if you are watching like a hawk and your entire being during the take is focused on what the actors and the camera are doing, it may well be that you notice something visually, and – if someone else is on the camera – you say to the camera person, 'I think if you started to move in slowly at the point that she says this, that'll help the scene.' The energy increases from the camera movement as well now, so you're now looking at all the key elements of cinema: camera movement, acting, how to use the light and everything. And your timing. And I would say in three or four takes in you've gone from what seemed to be complete disaster to something that clearly is going to work. Not only is it going to work, it's exciting and enjoyable, and by the end of the day everyone will leave with the real high of not just having got the scene but having enjoyed the working experience. Unless you create an environment where people enjoy the working experience, the chances of making a good film are minimal.

Engaging the Actors

In making my films, I've made it my business to make the actors feel engaged with the camera. I like being involved with the drama. So operating the camera puts me into the drama. And because I'm the director, not just a Director of Photography, I know that it has a tremendous effect on the actors. They feel that I'm right there, right in their face and they're acting to me. And so I always get a better performance. But then I'm a very hands-on director. That happens to be the system that is effective for me. And what I also do, when working on video, if I do a take and I really like it, I'll show it to the actors straight away, just on my camera. It's mildly ridiculous, in that you then get four or five actors crowded round a tiny three-inch screen. But it's enough for them to think, 'Wow, that looks good' – for them to understand what their work is translating as. I think that's the key thing. Some actors say they don't like to see themselves, but you need to see yourself because you need to see what the camera's doing. You need to be informed about what your possibilities are.

I don't like to rehearse too much. If I rehearse, I like the actors to use flat voices. I want to hear if the text works, and, if not, I'll make adjustments to the script. I have a real fear that if they engage emotionally in the rehearsal, when we come to shoot it they'll impersonate the rehearsal because they already did something interesting. So I like to get them excited in the rehearsal by the potential of what they could do, but I don't let them do it.

Acting *v.* Camera Movement

Even if I know it's going to be a technically complicated scene to shoot, to begin with I'll keep the actors quite flat, because what I'd hate is for them to do a great sequence and the camera wasn't quite ready for them. So always bear in mind these two parallel necessities: the acting and the technical camera movement. Familiarise yourself with everything in the room, so everyone has an idea of where they're going. Often, my voice will be very loud on an early take. I'll keep directing, knowing that there is still the correct energy and part of it will be usable. Often during a very important take I might speak. The actor might do something and it's really good and I'll just get into a different position and say, 'Do it again. I'll just get closer.' So I keep their juice going.

It's hard to explain, but the tone of your voice has to be appropriate to what they're doing. If you technically disassociate yourself from the drama and use a director's voice, you risk taking them out of the drama too. You might as well say 'Cut!' at that point. But if I'm going to keep shooting I might say, 'Yeah, that's good, that's really good. Push that idea. Go back on that line, but with more aggression.' I don't want to stop the camera and stop everybody and re-set – I know I'll definitely have to shoot a reverse in order to cut my voice out of all these pieces. But there is nothing like the moment when the camera is actually turning because that's when the actor is going to be most involved in the scene. To minimise the periods when the camera's turned off, because tape is cheap I'd rather just keep it running and do three takes without stopping.

The actor may not even look like the character you had in your mind, so you're already starting from the disadvantage that they're older or younger, darker or lighter. You had an idealised image, maybe a particular actor in mind, and then for various reasons you've got an actor who looks nothing like the character you envisaged. It's counterproductive to artificially impose your original vision. The best thing you can do is say: 'Okay, let's see what they can do.' And then, within their range, start adjusting towards what you want. The big mistake is to try to make actor B become actor C. They're not; they're individuals. There's no point putting them in the film unless you acknowledge that they're individuals. At the end of the day they are *themselves* playing someone else.

It's all about how adaptable you are. You learn over the years not to front-load the concept too much. Don't think too hard about what the actor looks like or what they sound like. Instead, you should be thinking that the story is this: it's a person, in a kind of industrial environment, in summer, but autumn would do as well. I'm not sure what the weather is; it's not so important. So don't overdress your framework before you get to reality, because if you do you'll always be disappointed. 'This is the situation, deal with it' – making a film is series of such occasions, every step of the way.

It goes back to Godard: 'Show me the budget and I'll show you the film.' Okay, I've got this much money. I'm going to go out shopping now and I'll get as many actors as I can get within this time frame. One of the things that has unhinged cinema to an extent is pre-planning something with all the limitations that go with singular vision. And then artificially reproducing them almost by force and by money. Like a big jet that takes off that, aerodynamically, is pretty crap. But with four very powerful engines and a shed-load of fuel, that plane will fly. Then there's the glider that, with a little bit of help, will just go using the wind. I think the difference between the two different types of filmmaking is very like that.

The ability to adapt to 'what is' goes back to my earlier statement that digital filmmaking has a lot more in common with documentary filmmaking than it has with traditional, conventional filmmaking.

9
Post-Production

A Disciplined Environment Is Crucial

You write a brilliant script set in the Bahamas, with scenes in the Sahara Desert and a climax outside the Old Bailey – it may be a great idea, but how on earth are you going to raise money for it? The alternative is to write a great script with a realistic story – that is, one that can be shot by raising a little bit of money, but not so much that you're middle-aged before you finally get to make the film.

In the same way, once you're shooting your realistic script you have to resist being extravagant, in order to be kind to yourself as the editor. On digital it's very tempting to just shoot from the hip with five cameras, because of the economy of the cameras and reusing tapes. But it can result in a complete nightmare – and I have experienced this – whereby you end up in an editing room with boxes and boxes of videotape, all of which have to be dealt with. In order to be kind to yourself in the final stages of post-production, you need to be doing some pretty stringent editing while you shoot.

There are two ways of doing it. One is by being very thorough on paper in your preparation for the shoot. Whether by storyboards or carefully thought-out shot-lists, you should conceive the progress of the film in detail, and then try to stick to that as much as possible as you shoot – allowing for the fact that great ideas will occur to you when you're filming. But in order for these ideas to have a chance of being born, avoid creative chaos on the set. There's a temptation – and I've seen it many, many times – where, even on a small crew, everyone has their own DV camera and they say, 'I've seen a great angle here', and they shoot it for you and you come away thinking, 'Wow, I've got so much coverage.' But then, when you try to make head or tail of the tapes, you find they haven't been marked up properly, and the shots don't really cut together because no one bothered to colour-balance the cameras.

Which brings us to the second thing you have to consider, which is colour-balance. That is something you have to do if you're shooting on video. You have to make sure that all of the cameras have the same menu settings – otherwise one beautiful shot may be very blue, and another beautiful shot may be very red. And short of reducing everything to black and white in post-production, it's extremely difficult to colour-balance one camera against another if their colour menu settings are so extremely apart. Even if they're on automatic, if you point a camera into the light the camera will automatically reset its colour-balance. If you then shoot with the light behind you, it will reset again. You must note this and acknowledge it. And it takes time.

In order to avoid these problems, you should be thinking about post-production during the shooting stage. You should decide, 'I'm really going to be quite stringent, almost military about this, and restrict my options. When I shoot this scene, there's going to be one camera, and maybe two cameras for *that* scene. And then if there's a scene involving a stunt, then fine, three or four cameras can only be useful . . .'

If you have restricted yourself to this kind of discipline

then it will not only be possible for a great idea to emerge, but you'll also have the space to make it work. In that kind of Spartan environment you find there's *room* for that new idea. And I'd go as far as to say that if you restrict your vision to, say, one form, as you preconceive it the day or the week before you shoot it, with the idea that the function of this approach is to allow on-set creativity to take place, then it *will* happen. But it can only happen in a disciplined environment. There are too many things to eat up time on a low-budget shoot – if you don't plan it, if you don't have the discipline, you'll end up running out of time *all* the time.

The Good Clerk

One thing that is *absolutely* essential for post-production is the clerical aspect of digital filmmaking. For all its freedoms – its ease of movement, the lightness and cheapness of equipment, the availability of the stock, all these wonderful factors that have liberated the filmmaking process – if there is not one person on set whose sole function is to help the editor by having a meticulously maintained book which is a log of everything that is being shot, then you will have chaos. And related to that log, *every* tape has to have a label on it, a colour code to say which camera it's from. And you need a detailed shot-list. The imposition of this discipline on the camera operators is of fundamental importance. If they're not bullied into doing it, it won't happen.

If you come from a traditional film background, the discipline exists: that of looking after the camera, cleaning the lens, logging the shots, being sure the batteries are charged, knowing that the tapes are all prepared with blank labels on them, the uniformity of labelling so every tape has a number and a date and a reference to a log which will give a full description of every shot and its duration. If you don't do this, you will have the following situation: there's a wrap party, and everybody's euphoric in the belief that they have a masterpiece in their hands. But the editor has had a look at the cardboard boxes containing maybe three hundred fiddly little tapes, and he's starting to realise that there's no clerical editing system, and what he's got to do first, in real time, is go through every single tape and log it, just to see if it's even worth having as part of his repertoire. He'll have to come up with a completely new filing system so he can find those tapes. And then go through the process of digitising them.

I can't stress this enough: the most important thing in digital filmmaking is logging. The sadness is that if you haven't logged properly then certain brilliant shots are never going to be seen.

A Different Way of Crewing

The traditional function of key people within the filmmaking process really has not been challenged in the last fifty years. You have a director, you have an assistant director, you have a continuity person, you have hair and make-up and so on. And you have an editor. An editor on a 35mm film is somebody who, while you're shooting, is preparing the rushes and organising their projection daily so that everyone can see what they shot the day before. The editor has looked at that footage and become familiar, to a certain degree, with what's been shot – certainly with all of the stuff that's been marked to print. I've tried in the past to involve them further. I've said, 'What do you think of this scene?' And they always say that they value being asked for an opinion, but I've never really felt it's been a 100 per cent commitment to being part of the process. They see their function as being post-production, which, in an obvious sense, it is.

But for a low-budget, digital film I would suggest a different way of crewing. In digital filmmaking I would say the function of the editor should be to be onboard from day one of the shoot. The editor should be the person on set – or the editor's assistant, certainly someone from the editing department – who makes sure that the footage is being issued and catalogued in a way that they understand. Also, the tapes should be viewed on a daily basis, in the way that 35mm used to be viewed. So that when a tape gets put into a box they have some idea of what has been shot.

When we shot *Hotel* I didn't have an editor onboard, but I did have people whose responsibility it was to take the footage on a daily basis and start digitally copying it and putting it into some form of hard drive. If the editing department can be the people during a digital shoot who are logging everything, then by the time the film has wrapped, everything has been logged already. And that is a bonus, because the process of logging is interminable.

Logging

What happens is this. You have recorded your master shot on a very small plastic tape – and it makes professionals who have worked in the business for a long time *very* insecure when you pick up this thing that could be crushed with one hand. If you dropped it and stood on it by accident, you would have destroyed the master tape. It's a vulnerable piece of plastic. People are used to big metal cans containing thick, heavy film – negative – and there's a substance to that. But, just as cameras have got smaller, obviously the things that we record in the cameras have got smaller. So the general consensus now is that the smart thing to do is copy this film, and by 'copy' I mean clone it – actually duplicate it. In the days of analogue, if you made a copy of something you lost a generation of quality. On a sound tape you would increase white noise. On a piece of imagery you would increase the grain structure. But digital information is digital information, and when you clone it digitally, you literally copy all of the yes/no interludes, and the result is a perfect copy. Theoretically, you can copy it as many times as you like. So this means that it's okay to take your master and reproduce it on to a stronger format.

At the moment, the stronger format is Digital Beta tape. This is expensive and the equipment that it is played on is also very expensive. But it does create some kind of insurance of the original material, which would be required by a financier, for instance, because it would be far too vulnerable to have just this one source as the sole copy of the film. So you copy it on to a digital piece of tape. And from then on, the manipulation of the image is done from this much stronger, bigger, more substantial cassette. The original masters that are on DV are then supposedly put into a climate control vault somewhere where there's not going to be a fire. What one needs to do – and very few people do this – is to separate the master and the clone immediately. The truth is that if you go into most editing rooms, the mas-

116

ters will be on one shelf and the digital clones on another. The chances of a fire are minimal, but it would be awful if that happened.

The good news is that digital material, theoretically, can be reused. So you can very cheaply acquire second-hand Digital Beta tapes that have been wiped, and then reuse them. And they ought to be as good as a new one. I do that myself. I refuse to buy new stock each time, so I will use the cassette for a couple of generations, unless there's some problem.

Duplicating is a real-time process so if you have a one hour tape, to make a copy of it takes one hour plus whatever time it takes to put the tape in, label it and so on. For an hour's footage, you should allow an hour and a half.

All of this is on the assumption that some sort of vetting and assessment of the material has taken place, and a good logging system used. And a good logging system means that when you get down to the finer points of editing and you need a shot that has *this* angle, you just open your log and you say, 'Actually, yes, we didn't digitise this shot originally but we've got it on tape six. And it'll work for five seconds as a cutaway.' But if you don't know where that is, it's a nightmare. Some poor bastard has to go through five hours of footage to find one cutaway.

So then the logging process begins. Once again, it's a real-time process. One hour of footage to be imported into a hard drive of a computer takes one hour plus whatever time it takes to program the computer. At this point, you have two choices. If you're going to use the computer as the mastering device for the finished film, you have to take in the tape that you are importing into the computer at the highest possible resolution, at broadcast-quality resolution. The simple rule is, the higher the resolution, the more hard drive space the image uses up. And imagery takes up a huge amount of hard drive. Sound, virtually nothing. But imagery at its highest resolution means that you are – on a feature-length film and at a ratio of hypothetically 10:1 – looking at maybe fifteen to twenty hours of high resolution imagery, recorded on not just one drive but many drives. Very few people will have such a collection of hard drives, so what most people do is rent drives.

Renting is cheaper but can be frustrating, because as soon as you give the drives back, the imagery you've stored on those drives is going to be wiped. Then if you need to pick up a shot, you're going to have to go through the process again of importing the original shot. Having said that, it's not so difficult, because even though the drives would be wiped of the actual material, the memory of it is retained via the EDL – the Edit Decision List, which is basically a menu of every single shot that you put into the computer, with the start point, the number of the tape, the end point of the tape, and the duration of the shot. If you've wiped a shot but you've retained your EDL then all you have to do is put the tape back in and within the tape programme it says 'Import this shot' and you highlight it and the video machine and the computer will just speak to each other. It will automatically find that shot and import it for you.

It's better to own your drives because then six months later the information will still be sitting there if you want to make some changes. On the other hand, as a discipline it's not a bad idea to get into the habit of wiping your drives regularly, because otherwise you just end up with lots and lots of drives with information that you somehow can't bear to part with.

The Process of Editing

When all your information is housed in a central computer, the editor can begin editing. The beauty of the digital editing system is that, with the help of some drives, you could theoretically be on set with a laptop and maybe one extra screen, and while the shooting is taking place you could be importing the footage from the day before, or even from that same morning. And by ten o'clock that night there's really nothing that would have stopped you cutting the scene together. They say 'in rough form', but nothing is rough now on a computer. The way people cut on computers is as if it's always the final cut. Of course, it can change and get shorter later on, but it would be an interesting discipline if that happened.

I did a master-class in Slovenia where I had two editors and I insisted they come in with laptops for the editing process. When I got there I discovered they had been rather underhand and demanded full desk set-ups. They didn't want to sit there with a laptop. There was a kind of arrogance about that which pissed me off, because the whole function of the exercise was to show the portability of the equipment – plus I liked the idea of the editors working in the same environment, not doing their traditional thing of hiding themselves away in some cell somewhere. It would be very good for the actors – and for the director too – if instead of the traditional method of looking at uncut dailies, at the end of each day we would be looking at cut scenes from the day before. From an acting point of view you would really get a sense of how you're being treated, how you're being photographed, and a sense of what the director's and the editor's psychology for the story is, which is something that can only emerge when you see the scenes cut together.

From the editor's point of view, they can't really give you a judgement on the footage that's being delivered to them until they cut it. They always say, 'It looks good, it'll cut well.' And then when you start cutting with them they say, 'Oh, didn't you do a reverse?' And you go, 'No, you saw the stuff I shot. Why didn't you spot that I didn't do a reverse?'

It used to be that you'd often see the credit 'Writer-Director', but hardly ever 'Director-Editor'. It's much more common now. A lot of filmmakers have come up through editing. It's a curious process, handing the film over to somebody else's eye in post-production. It's quite frustrating if you are the kind of director that wants to be actively involved in the process all the way. Most of the young directors that I've met are totally familiar with things like Final Cut Pro or Avid and have cut together their own films. And now with film students, it would be very rare – though it is still taught in some film schools – to be taught to cut on a Steenbeck flatbed editing table. Pretty much everyone has their laptop and some form of editing system software, and they do their own. So they're much more familiar and less intimidated by the procedure of editing.

Are Editors Necessary?

It's good to have an editor to work with in post-production. But there are certain things to be aware of. One is your own laziness. You've just come through a shoot, you're probably quite exhausted, and this raises issues immediately. The editor's eye will not be the same as your eye. Some editors regard their job as fixing the problems that the poor unfortunate director created because they didn't really know what they were doing. They will make decisions – as a cinematographer would on set – to give the best possible technical cut, which nevertheless may not use the take that contains what is, emotionally, the best performance.

It's very easy to go into an almost narcoleptic state in post-production. You're in a dark room, you're suddenly inactive, and you're sitting next to someone who's obsessively looking at screens. It's a mesmerising environment. The temptation is to go to sleep a lot of the time, certainly to go into a low-energy state. And being in that environment for years and years does start to have an effect on people. Editors have personalities too. It's vitally important that you don't lose the plot in the editing room, that you stay aggressively involved in the film. You can't just abdicate your responsibility. I've found in many instances when a film is finally finished and it's out there, I suddenly remember a shot that I did and I think, 'Oh my god, I never even saw it in post-production.' That was probably the result of there being so much footage that just dealing with what the editor was constantly confronting me with took all my energy. I went off the boil. I lost my focus. If the editor's really good, it may not matter because they will have taken over that focus for you. But it's important that you keep your own focus in post-production.

For instance, let's say you've created a good environment for organic creativity while you're shooting because your template was fairly simple and you left enough space and time. And you come up with something at a complete tangent to what was in the script – wacky stuff that makes sense in *your* mind. However, when that footage turns up and the person who is editing compares what's in the script with what you've shot, they'll say, 'Wow, this is interesting stuff but I've got no idea where it's coming from.' So there needs to be communication between the two of you. The best thing would be to try to cut that material, and if it cuts well it would indicate a new direction for the film. However, if it's just shelved, then by the time you look at it a month later you may remember having been excited by it, but the impetus has been lost. There are so many other things pushing you in a more conventional direction that you may lose your enthusiasm for it or be intimidated out of trying to put it in the cut. All these things lead back to an essential discipline, which is that it's not enough to have a good vision and an inventive flair unless you are able to catalogue your information into some kind of structure. If you don't, then it will never make it into the film.

The Equipment

The big breakthrough in digital post-production and the use of computers was when Lightworks and Avid first appeared on the scene, and people started to take them seriously. I remember that on *The Sheltering Sky* (1990) Bertolucci used a complex bank of videotape recorders, all with different tapes in them. At that time computers didn't have the sort of storage possibility they have now, so this was basically what is called an offline system: you took a low-resolution copy of the film into the computer, you cut with that, and then the EDL – that list of all the in-points and out-points – was used in the way that a conventional 35mm cutter would take the numbers off the negative and cut the film. So you edited on computer for, let us say, the physical ease and exploration of this new technology. But the back end of that was that the actual cutting of the film and the creation of the final cut was through the traditional means of neg cutting.

Over the last ten years, the storage of computer information has accelerated to such an extent that you can take in a film or a videotape at the highest resolution, as good as the original, and store that on the computer. So now you're cutting with high-definition quality. Once you cut it, even on a simple laptop or Mac, you are cutting something as if you're cutting the negative. Which means that when you finally cut it together, all you need to do is export the finished result, which would consist of a couple of thousand edits and sound dissolves and so on. Once you've done that – and it's very complex, there's two tracks for the visual and maybe ten tracks for the sound and so on – you can export it as a single package. One cut. And that final cut, which is exported to Digital Beta tape – or to a DVD, which would be lower resolution – is of broadcast quality. It is of the same high quality as the original tape from which those images were taken. As far as sound is concerned – and you can now do your digital sound post-production on software like Final Cut Pro or Avid – the mix which you've done in your computer is a good mix. So at this lowest possible level of finance, just by renting a few hard drives you have the ability to professionally post-produce and finish your film on your laptop or your desk set-up. Export it, and what you've exported is the finished result.

Two Routes

At this point the film can be digitally transferred on to 35mm negative, and you can make a 35mm print which has been sourced from your computer; or it can go to any other digital format. It can be in a cinema as either a digital projection or, with a bit more time and money, as conventional 35mm. All the Dogme films and any other recent films that have been shot on video would have gone through that process.

If people *want* at that point to spend a lot of money, they can go to a post-production house with incredibly sophisticated equipment and take those same shots that are in their computer, export the whole thing, and then colour-correct it visually. But then you can do that in your laptop too. The only advantage in a post-production house is that the monitors you are looking at are scientifically balanced so there's a consistency of colour and so on, and obviously a far greater range of subtlety in terms of the grading of the film. In the same way, you can export all of your tracks – they're digital clones – as a multi-track file and take it to a sound post-production house and do a professional mix as you would on a feature film with a huge sound stage, which is what I did with *Timecode*.

I've done the entirely home product, where everything is done on one computer with a pair of small but decent speakers and a high-quality domestic monitor. And then I've done the other route, which is to take all of my components once they've been cut and go to two different places: one is a visual post-production place, and the other is a sound post-production place. And once both of those facility houses have done their bit, the finished results are married together digitally and then I can have either a 35mm print or a digital print.

The Difference between Film and Digital Projection

One of the really stupid elements of the system that we now find ourselves in – which in years to come will, I'm sure, seem so absurd to any film student as to be unbelievable – is that, for reasons that are not even worth going into, film projection is at twenty-four frames a second while video records at twenty-five frames a second. It still seems to be a huge challenge to modify the system so both of them run at the same speed. At present, when you're transferring your lovely digital film on to film negative, it runs at a different speed. *Hotel* was shot on digital, and when it's projected on film it's one twenty-fifth of a second slower – so the film runs longer by three minutes, and the score is transposed down a semitone. And people's voices drop a semitone, which for voices is okay. The reverse used to happen when you transferred a film on to tape: the voices and the score went up a semitone, so everything was just a little bit faster and the voices had a slightly more Mickey Mouse quality.

This problem doesn't exist in America because American video shoots at thirty frames a second and they use a system of drop frames, so the transfer is the same length and there is no loss in sound pitch or anything like that. It's only in Europe with the PAL standard where you have twenty-five versus twenty-four. The answer would be to convert all projectors to the same speed as the video equipment. All film cameras pretty much have a twenty-four/twenty-five FPS possibility because once it became clear that movie cameras were being used for television all camera manufacturers put a switch on those cameras that enables you to shoot at either twenty-four or twenty-five frames a second. But there isn't a conversion switch on video. There are systems of digital conversion that convert twenty-five to twenty-four, but the problem there is that any panning shots tend to strobe for some reason. So until we move over to a purely digital system, the problem only exists when we have to transfer to film. If you shoot digitally and project digitally, it will be fine.

Time to Think

A number of established filmmakers resisted digital editing initially because they used the time in which the editing assistant was hunting through the trims in order to think about what they were doing. But I think younger filmmakers who have grown up with digital would argue, 'Well, I could cut four versions in that same time and show you the options.' Or we could just stop and have a cup of tea and think about it.

Does 'time to think' have to be the result of the inefficiency of a system? Or can it be something which people think is a good idea in itself, in the form of built-in breaks? I think these *are* a good idea, because one of the real problems with digital post-production is that the editor becomes a zombie, just staring at these screens all day.

They don't even look at you when they're talking because they're constantly fiddling with the mouse. I've had situations where I've actually said, 'Do you mind? When we speak, can you look at me? And – I'm sorry to say this – can you take your hand off the mouse?' But then the hand creeps back to the mouse because it's become their life. They're constantly moving their hand and trying things and dragging things out of bins and so on. And they get really good at it. It's like an addiction to computer games.

So it's quite a good idea to say, 'Okay, every hour and a half we stop for ten minutes and go outside and take some air. And discuss something away from the screen, and then come back.' It's really up to individuals to impose forms of discipline on the system that create space to think – because if you don't make that happen, the system itself will not throw up those kind of thinking breaks.

iMovie *v.* Final Cut Pro

When you buy a Mac, it automatically comes with iMovie Plus, which is a slightly more sophisticated version of iMovie based on the fact that people really liked the system and used it, and decided they wouldn't mind just a few more variations. Capitalism being what it is, other computer companies are also trying to offer a few more bells and whistles. What was called Something becomes Something Plus, and its next generation is Super-Plus 2 and so on.

My experience with iMovie was interesting. I had it on my computer and I never used it. Then, one day, I shot something that I didn't really want anybody else to cut at that stage. I just wanted to look at it. And I had no idea how to use the iMovie system. I am not someone who could be described as computer literate. I don't love computers. I have been dragged to them reluctantly, and have then been delighted by what they can do, but I had some difficulty in learning the systems initially. So I would say I represent the low end of capability here. Compared to anyone under thirty, who will have had far more experience with computers than I have ever had, I'm in the Stone Age. So I turned the system on and there was a little demo reel that came with it just to help one through the process. I found out how to plug in my camera so that I could use the camera as a playback machine and as an importing machine. That seemed very straightforward.

Then I started importing some shots, and I saw very quickly how they aligned themselves into a sort of catalogue. Within a couple of hours I'd cut a sequence. I started to think about how I could do a little sound dissolve here, and I went into the menu that said what was available in terms of effects for sound and effects for visuals. And it was so obvious and so self-explanatory, even to a novice like me, that I cut a really rather sophisticated five-minute film. Starting from zero, I did it in one day. And I immediately thought I could cut a whole feature like this.

When I shot my first film I got a friend who was a filmmaker to agree to edit it. When I saw the result I was horrified and distressed by what he'd done to my footage. I found it hard to disguise that. I was trying to be tactful but he got rather upset and just said, 'Well, cut it yourself then.' But he said it in a nice way. He had an editing room and he said, 'We use it in the daytime, but if you don't mind cutting at night or when we're on holiday, you can edit here.' And he threw me into the room. I had never, ever edited a film. I had no experience. And it was a Steenbeck, so I had to learn how to synchronise the film, and I taught myself Steenbeck editing in that way. It was the state-of-the-art editing machine for 35mm, but the choices available were that one piece of celluloid, with the image, could be put on it and then, depending on how expensive your Steenbeck was, you could either have one, two, three or even four sound-tracks. So you could end up with four rolls of celluloid on a film, three of which were sound. And I would say that iMovie is far more sophisticated than any Steenbeck I've ever seen.

You could never do a dissolve on a Steenbeck. You couldn't do a sound mix. Basically, all you could do was show the film, then pull it out and, literally, cut it yourself. But if you wanted to do a dissolve you used to have to put pencil marks on to the celluloid. With iMovie, if you want a five-second mix you hit a button and it takes a very short amount of time to conform and show you the mix. So on the day when I cut my five-minute film it was mind-boggling to think I could do sound, fade in and out, and by the end of it I thought, 'Wow. Really, if I'm honest, that's the kind of filmmaking I'm interested in.'

The digital quality on iMovie is first class, exactly the same as Final Cut Pro. Even though Final Cut has got millions more options, the end result of editing on iMovie is a broadcast-quality piece of film through a very simple system. If this was 1965 and iMovie suddenly came on the market it would be regarded as a complete breakthrough in post-production. Now, because there are so many other systems out, it's sort of regarded as a bit of a joke. I remember talking to Terry Gilliam about it and he said to me very quietly, 'Have you tried iMovie?' And I said, 'Yeah.' He said, 'It's great, isn't it?' And I said, 'It's fantastic.' We were admitting that we thought it was an amazing piece of software, but we were both furtively looking around in case any other film people were near us.

The other advantage is that once you've taught yourself on iMovie, the logical transition to the fundamental stage of Final Cut Pro, the more sophisticated system, is very straightforward. My advice about both these systems would be, 'Use them for what you need them for. Don't feel like you need to use the full range of their menu, because it's vast.'

The limitation of iMovie is that you can have two soundtracks, maybe three. But when you go to Final Cut Pro, you can have as many as you like – twelve, twenty soundtracks going at the same time, exactly as you would on a professional film mix. And so I cautiously entered the more sophisticated system. And each time I needed to do something – slow this section down into a slo-mo, or distort the image a little bit – then I would just stop and go into the menu and I'd look at the effects and just try it. The great thing is that you try something and if you don't like it you just hit Apple-x or Apple-z and it takes you back to before you tried that effect, so you can try something else or keep it as it is.

With these systems, the first question is: how do I just cut a piece of film? In fact it's very, very easy. If you want to do something a bit more complicated, then you start spending time or asking someone else, or just patiently going into the menu. There is a good design logic that has gone into these systems because in many instances they have evolved, surprisingly, out of amateur filmmaking. You can make a film like this. *Tarnation* was completely edited on iMovie, and everybody who's seen the film has been very satisfied with the result.

The Importance of Sound Quality

I've always said you can shoot on any camera as long as you get an interesting image, an interesting composition or interesting use of colour. With one kind of camera, you think: 'What's good about this camera is that it gives a kind of funky look, so I'm going to shoot it in a funky kind of way.' Or maybe there's a clinical look to the camera which will suggest a different shooting style. The resolution of the image can be very low, very pixellated and full of grain, but that in itself can be a visually exciting element. All that is fine. What is really important and I think *not* negotiable, is that if you are intending your film to be seen by other people at a venue for, say, a hundred people, the sound quality has to be fantastic. If it sounds big like a film, then you can get away with any kind of visual style. But the sound of the voices and the music and the quality of the mix need to be of the highest possible level. And with digital technology, that is possible. You can achieve that kind of mix on a laptop, as long as you're listening on good headphones or reasonably good monitor speakers.

On *Timecode* – where you have four parallel stories on four screens – the key element to the film was the sound edit. It was going to be the thing leading the audience through the narrative. Everyone who has seen *Timecode* has said to me that they had imagined the experience of watching it would be very confusing, and they were really surprised that it wasn't difficult to watch at all, because the sound was very, very clear. The story moved with the soundtrack, so although it was moving from screen one to screen four and back to screen three, what helped you follow where the story was going was the sound mix.

Even with a single screen you still have to recognise how important the sound is. Consistently over the past few years people have complained: 'I'm sure it's an interesting film, but I really couldn't hear what anyone was saying.' The rain was too loud; the effects people went mad with the explosions; or the music was wall-to-wall, drowning everything out.

You need to get the sound right in the shooting. Even though you're shooting on digital cameras, you need to spend the correct amount of time on where the microphones are placed. And don't start until you've got good sound, otherwise you're shooting yourself in the foot. You might have an interesting visual, but if the sound doesn't work you're going to have to loop it and that's never a great thing to do on a film, because you have taken one level of reality away.

10
Music

The Psychological Backbone

My theory of film music is that the essential psychology of a film is supplied by music. It functions as a psychological backbone. In fact, some filmmakers self-consciously avoid using music for this very reason: they don't want the emotional climate of the film to be dictated by the music.

Here is an interesting fact: if you don't put any music on your film, then after a while people don't miss it. The minute you put thirty seconds of music on to the film, it's almost as if you've crossed a line that you can't reverse: the audience will then expect more music.

There are two obvious ways to address this phenomenon. One is to put almost wall-to-wall music on the film – which is a mistake that many filmmakers make, not only as first-time directors but thirtieth-time directors too. It seems to arise from a feeling of insecurity that the film can't speak for itself or that the audience may be bored. It's a problem of addiction – the more music you put in, the more demanding it becomes. In order to maintain any sense of excitement you constantly have to increase the amount of music, to a disproportionate degree. Instead I would say that the use of music should be minimal, sparing.

Films *are* made without any music at all, and they can be very powerful and effective – but, in general, we expect music. And having finished a film, all filmmakers at the outset of their career have to confront the expectation that there will be music on it somewhere. So what are your choices?

Ready-Made Music

One is to use existing music, as typified by teen movies that use a lot of pop songs, which are known as 'needle-drops'. Interestingly, a lot of contemporary musicians working within the pop music genre are writing music that is very influenced by film, almost like atmospheric music, and which, clearly, would work well *within* a film. So, within the huge range of what exists in recorded music now, there is a big choice of music and genre. But if you use a song by Radiohead or the Beatles or whoever, these are very expensive – you have to buy them, obtain a licence to use them in your film. But there is another choice. If you happen to know a really good rock band who are looking for a deal, then you can satisfy each other by saying, 'I'll put you on my soundtrack if you license your music to me for a nominal amount, and then we can also make a CD of the soundtrack and do a profit-share on that.'

One problem with pre-existing music is that it's not really flexible. But with digital post-production, it's possible to manipulate existing pieces of music. You can re-edit a piece so that it works dynamically and emotionally with the piece of film that you've cut.

Because the pop industry is an incredibly saturated business where far too much music is recorded and released on a weekly basis, the executives are constantly looking for alternative outlets, and film is a real target for them. Therefore any young filmmaker will be able to get an interview with a record company, particularly if it's an indie label. They will be enthusiastic and will probably send you many CDs to listen to. And they'll make a deal for the song you want – but at the same time they'll try to offload a lot of rather second-rate music on to you as well: 'If you want this track, then you've got to take *these* tracks . . .' I've suffered from this in the past.

With any existing music, you have to ask yourself a very honest question: 'Does this piece of music happen to exactly fit a scene that I've already cut? Or am I cutting or extending this scene to make it fit to a piece of pop music, which will be great on the soundtrack album?' It's not uncommon to see films these days where nothing's happening apart from a rather banal pop song, which in a year's time is going to be as dated as flared trousers.

Library Music

Library music is basically pre-recorded mood music, written by film composers for a specific kind of sequence – a thrilling sequence, or a tragic-romantic one, or a farcical one, whatever it may be. The titles of these pieces tend to be bizarre: 'A Summer Day in Crete', or 'Terror in Haunted House'. Obviously, they have to be so literal in order that you can look them up in an index and have a very clear idea of what you're going to get. This too is music that you still have to license, but it's cheaper than going to a composer – and the other thing is, it's ready-made.

A Unique Sound

The creative alternative to pre-recorded music is to work with a gifted musician to create an original score for your film – which means that your film will have a unique voice.

What makes matters difficult is that you are handing over the psychological thrust of the film to someone who is coming in at the final stage of post-production – unless the composer happens to have been around from the very beginning. With most films music is one of the very last stages: the film is cut and the dialogue is in place and so on, and then the music is put in. But it's then a very delicate subject – this decision about when the music comes into the film and starts having a powerful relationship with the audience.

Temp Scores

A temp score is where the filmmaker has had the unfortunate idea of borrowing a score done by John Williams or Ennio Morricone or another composer. In other words, they have bought a very inexpensive collection of CDs of the most powerful, popular film scores available, and put these on their film. And the film suddenly seems real and works really well. And then you have the tactless situation of the filmmaker saying to the composer, 'Of course this is just the temp score, but I'd like it to sound like this piece by Morricone . . .' The composer is already offended because he's being asked to impersonate something that already exists, which he probably has contempt for anyway – because if a composer is interesting he will already be thinking beyond what's already been done by other composers in the past. So that is a real danger – falling in love with a score that you can't have. If it's an existing score, you won't be able to get it, and nor really should you want to.

My advice is that if you are going to go the route of having a temp score, be as minimal as possible. And if you already have a relationship with a composer, make up the temp score from something the composer has previously done, so you're allowing that composer the time to experiment with the film. These days, just by using keyboards and string samples you can make a very convincing score yourself until you're happy with the psychological relationship between the film and the music.

A Musical Background

To me, the most productive route is working with a composer. And if you're making cutting-edge digital films, you should be looking at cutting-edge digital scoring – in exactly the same way as you made the decision about who's going to be shooting your film and who's going to be acting in it. It's not arbitrary. These are very precise decisions, to be made after a lot of thought and observation.

Let's say you're making your first feature. Your musical experience might be anything from the minimal – everybody likes music so they'll have some taste and know what they like, what makes them laugh or cry or whatever – to that of the small percentage of filmmakers who have a working understanding of music. They might understand how music is made. That could range from their playing the piano or another instrument themselves, to their perhaps having studied music. I didn't start out as a filmmaker myself, I started as a musician. Although I lacked formal background, I did manage to go to a college that produced music teachers. So I came out as a qualified music teacher, with a vast enthusiasm for music and some basic understanding of harmonic structure, as well as the spiritual basis of music.

One of the great film composers, Morricone, formulated a list of advice to filmmakers and composers. He advised that you should not change the key of your piece of music unless you have a really good reason to – because when you change the key, it makes the audience think something else has changed. The function of music is to *underscore*. We use the word 'score', but what we really mean is 'underscore'. The score should not lead but support the film, adding tension and emotional subtlety. It is *under* the film. I have a huge problem with a lot of scores that I hear, which are definitely not under – they are *over* the film.

Morricone also advised to worry less about harmonic complexity and think more about combinations of sounds. Famously, for Sergio Leone's spaghetti Westerns he put a string section together with a jaw's harp, or an electric guitar or a banjo. He took the conventional structure of film music and then inserted voices that had a very distinctive connection with the visual elements of the film itself. In *Once Upon a Time in the West* he used a very simple harmonica phrase that became one of the dramatic points of the film. Basically, what he did was to take the conventions of the American TV Western with lots of galloping music and then put that into a slightly more sophisticated and modern context. So his music still sounds, to me, very modern. Also, he was not frightened of using a beautiful, simple melody – something that's rather gone out of favour with films. A lot of contemporary scoring is just about texture; there's a resistance to using tunes and thematic ideas, which used to be the basis of a score.

There's a famous story about a studio chief in the late '40s or '50s who went to a screening of a film and hated the score so much that he asked somebody afterwards, 'This *sound* that I keep hearing, what is it?' And eventually someone said, 'It's a minor chord.' He went off in a huff and the next day, posted all over the studio, was a diktat saying, 'From now on, no minor chords in any of my films.' Which, interestingly enough, is what Hitler said also when he banished jazz and Jewish music – one of the reasons given was that it was predominantly in the minor key. It was a depressing, moaning kind of music, and for a vibrant new culture everything should be in march-time and in a major key. Ironically, this studio chief came to the same conclusion when it came to the marketing of his films.

How to Discuss Music

For a filmmaker with little musical knowledge, it is very intimidating to suddenly have to have a quite grown-up discussion with a musician/composer about what they want in their film and what they need from the music. Which is why young filmmakers tend to put themselves totally in the hands of the composer and just say, 'Listen, here's some temp score that I really like. Over to you . . .' They feel a real sense of inferiority in talking about these things, as a result of not understanding them at all.

What can go disastrously wrong is that you go to a recording session and hear some music – and it might not be exactly what you had in mind, but it sounds impressive and it suddenly makes the film seem like a film. Then from scene to scene, the music is laid on, and each time you look at and listen to a 5- or 10-minute scene the music seems to work really well. But then when you hear the whole 90-minute film, with scene following scene following scene without a break, the music sounds monotonous, and has begun to lose its impact. Lacking the tools to discuss *why* it's not working, most filmmakers will say, 'I don't know, it's just not working for me.' And the composer will ask, 'Well, what do you *want*?' But it's much easier to say what you *don't* want when you really don't know how to articulate what you *do* want.

If we accept that music has become so important in contemporary film, then surely there is an argument for your being duty-bound to spend some time understanding music, even if that just means going to five one-hour lessons – exactly in the way you spend time trying to understand how a camera works, or the techniques of acting. I can guarantee that in five hours I could teach any filmmaker enough about music for them to understand how a score works and what are their choices in that area.

I would say the following items would be very, very useful in terms of the basic ability of film directors to discuss music:

1. Be able to tell the difference between minor and major keys.
2. Know a bit about modal music. Modal music basically

stays in one key and has very simple but subtle shifts of harmony within one tonality – much more like Indian music or Eastern music in general.

3. Understand a bit about voicing. Voicing is the effect whereby if you put this instrument with that instrument then you get a certain kind of colour.

Music is such an evolved form of the arts that its potential for ironic comment is colossal. Even an untrained audience understands the ironic potential of music. Let's say we have a scene where something dramatic has happened – a death, for instance. You could go to the library and ask for tragic-death music, and you'd be given several choices, all pretty much the same, labelled 'Tragic Death'. An alternative would be to go completely to the opposite end of the spectrum and use a piece of music that is light and romantic and gives us a kind of déjà vu of something much earlier in the character's life, which may trigger in the audience a far greater emotional response *because* it's light and ironic. This would throw the focus on to the acting, assuming the acting has been good. The music would be supporting the drama of the performance, rather than swamping it.

The problem of swamping is a real issue. If an actor does a really strong performance on his or her deathbed and it's tremendously moving, the tendency is to say, 'Okay, let's make it even more powerful by putting some music on.' That's when the danger signals should start flashing because if you put on powerful death music, you will of course move the audience but you also have to acknowledge the following: the audience may be moved by the music rather than by the performance and you will therefore have failed in your job of underscoring. So what you want is something that lifts the performance even higher by lifting it from underneath, so that the performance is even more visible. This can be done through very subtle use of what we call a string pad, which is just two notes played very softly with a delicate little phrase – either sung or played on the piano – but just occasionally put in, so that it never interferes with the dialogue. It's often a question of listening to the dialogue as if it were a vocal line and putting on enough of a string pad just to lift the performance and give it a bit more emotional intensity. And then, occasionally, to remind the audience the music is playing, use a very simple phrase, but do it in such a way that you never interfere with the dialogue.

Making the Orchestration Personal

In mainstream movies, a composer will look at the film, make some rough notes, and then go off and formally compose some music. But this music tends to have a general application to the scene, not a specific one. One of the things that I've loved doing over the years is making the orchestrating personal.

For example, in *Leaving Las Vegas* I had no money for the score, so I was using keyboards and samples and then a small group of very good improvisational jazz musicians. There's a moment in the film where Nicolas Cage goes to the bank and he's looking at an attractive blonde teller, and he goes into something like a '60s Beat poem: 'Do I find you attractive? Maybe if you poured whisky all over your breasts . . .' This poem is quite an important story point, and when we were recording the dialogue, Nicolas did a little musical sound with his voice. So when I did the score that would accompany this Beat poem, I asked the saxophonist to particularly watch out for this phrase, and then he echoed it. In fact I put the saxophone phrase in first so it sounded like Nicolas Cage was listening to a band and then impersonating the sound. It suddenly put the score into a position of being almost like live music, almost like there was a little trio playing behind Cage in the bank. That works specifically for that scene.

In 1955, Miles Davis was brought in on a Louis Malle film called *Elevator to the Gallows*. He watched the film, and he played live to it. And that has now become one of the seminal moments in jazz film scoring. It was pure film music – and it defined a new kind of cool jazz, with the music staying in one key. If you follow Miles Davis's career from this point onwards his music immediately becomes much simpler. One can argue that it was the influence of doing a film score that made him think, 'This is a more interesting way to go as a musician.' So these things do cross-fertilise, to the extent that film music as such has a wide listening and buying public. Any record store you go to has a soundtrack section. I think people like to listen to soundtracks as they drive – after all, we are in such a film culture. Equally you can listen to a band like Radiohead and think, 'This would work very well in film.' So I would say that it's worth exploring the avant-garde section of the pop scene, because it's there that you will find a big affinity for film, and for first-time digital filmmakers this is the talent pool where you might find the cutting edge of film composing today.

Keep Your Ears Clean

At the point in post-production when the music is introduced, it's very difficult to keep your ears fresh. You've seen the film so many times that it doesn't have the emotional impact that you expect it to have – and as a result, there's a danger of adding too much music. It's a law of diminishing returns. How many times can you watch a film anyway? Even with a classic, by the second or third viewing you're looking at things other than the plot. So you have to keep searching for ways to keep your ears clean, one of which is not to put too much music on in the first place.

What happens in America with mainstream films is that they test the film, and if it doesn't test very well, the first thing that will be blamed will be the music – hence the hysteria of adding louder and louder strings and making a bigger noise. Maybe the answer would be to take the music off altogether and then test the film, and afterwards start gently adding it back in.

Testing the Film

It's a good idea at regular intervals to screen the film to ten people in an informal environment, even on a computer screen with reasonable speakers in a room that's just dark enough. You will find that sitting with ten people who don't have a vested interest like your own will clean out your ears and eyes. As they concentrate on the film, you will see it a little bit through their experience; you will become aware of how they are reacting. And then allow enough time afterwards – at least an hour – and get some wine or coffee in and ask them, 'Okay, be honest. Were you bored?' There's no point in bringing your friends in and getting 'It's just great.' You have to be prepared to listen to their honest reactions. And you may by then have discovered some truths yourself by being with that audience.

Particularly with music, you'll hear when it becomes irritating or repetitive. On the question of variety and the ironic power of music, look at a film like *Le Mépris* by Godard. He basically got George Delerue to compose one piece of music – a rather hammy but beautiful romantic theme, quite unlike the music that Godard would normally use. And Godard being Godard, he chose to use that same piece of music about ten times in the film in different scenes with different impacts. And it becomes a tremendously powerful comment, almost like someone whistling the same tune. As an exercise in the understanding of what film score is and what it can do, it's worth looking at that film just to see what a master Godard is in the use of music, particularly the ironic use of music. I don't know of another filmmaker in the world who has the understanding of the power of music that Godard has.

Dealing with Studio Films

When you start off as a filmmaker you tend to have very clear ideas: shooting on DV, no lights, the smallest possible crew, etc. You become very tight, secure and comfortable with that system because it's a small team and everybody has a responsibility. So you make this film and it becomes *Blair Witch* and suddenly every studio in town wants to offer you a $60 million movie, and then you find yourself having to deal with what I've had to deal with – all the trucks and all the crap that comes with 35mm. And it takes away all your energy. A parallel situation exists in music.

Say you've done two or three features or documentaries. You've got a friend who's a really good cutting-edge musician who functions on the edge of the contemporary music scene and is a whiz with keyboards and understands film. So you use this sound and it becomes your trademark, and the way you use the camera works really well with this composer. Then suddenly there is enough money for a hundred musicians and a big recording studio, and you want to take the composer with you.

Now you have to deal with a vast number of musicians, and you have to make them as personal to your big feature film as your cool keyboard player was to your little DV film. This is much more difficult, and requires skill and an understanding of how best to use an orchestra and keep within the budget. And how to not be seduced by the fact that a hundred musicians are playing music that you or your friend wrote. What I've tried to do when I have that kind of a budget is to do exactly what I did on keyboards – which is to write a very minimal underscore. I'm very happy having thirty string players play one note or maybe two notes as quietly as possible because it's such a beautiful sound. It's something you can never really create on a keyboard by using loops. So, for the most part, I've not been fazed by the fact that fifty musicians are slightly bored by playing the same note for five minutes. All I want is the same kind of sound that I got on my keyboard.

Recycling

Sometimes a piece of music that was made specifically for one film can be used for one that is completely different in terms of genre. I played a piece of music to Nicolas Cage and Elisabeth Shue at the very beginning of the *Leaving Las Vegas* shoot and said, 'I'm going to use this music as your theme.' It was a theme I had written for Albert Finney, playing a retired Classics teacher at a British public school in *The Browning Version* – but it worked fine for *Leaving Las Vegas*. The moral is: be open to experiment, try things that don't necessarily seem the obvious choice.

The very minimal jazz trumpet score on *Leaving Las Vegas* originally appeared on an HBO film that I made called *Mara*, with Juliette Binoche. But it was taken off that film without any negotiation and replaced by one from another composer – and I felt that the music that ended up on that film was completely inappropriate. I had a rare moment of triumph when, after *Leaving Las Vegas* came out, I got a letter from David Brown, the producer of the HBO film with whom I had fallen out with because they'd re-edited the film and re-scored it. He said, 'I'm sure you'll be surprised to get a letter from me but I saw *Leaving Las Vegas* and I thought it was a wonderful film. Everything about it was great, the acting, everything. And I really liked the score.' So I wrote back saying that I was particularly touched that he liked the score and did he realise that it was the music he'd taken off the Juliette Binoche film? I never heard from him again.

11
Distribution

P&A

Once you step into the arena of filmmaking, because of the time and costs involved you have pretty much endorsed the idea that your film will go into a public domain and, one hopes, be seen by three or four hundred people at a sitting. In order for that to happen, you have to go through distribution. In fact, if you want people to see your film – as opposed to a poem or a personal drawing that stays in your notebook – then distribution is the most important aspect of filmmaking. And the problem with distribution is that when I find myself in the environment of young filmmakers and I say, 'Hands up who wants to be a distributor?', maybe one hand goes up. 'Who wants to be a producer?' More hands go up. 'Who wants to be a director?' Bang, everyone's hand is up.

The culture of film distribution is a complete mess. It's dominated by American studios who went out of their way in the past to buy up all the distribution chains, not only in America but in Britain and Europe. American studios produce too many films in the way that American car manufacturers produce too many cars and mobile phone makers produce too many phones. So the idea is to persuade people to constantly change their car and their mobile phone, and go and see another American film.

'P&A' stands for prints and advertising. The cost of prints is relatively small, but on a typical studio picture the budget of the film is often doubled by the advertising the studio feels is necessary to get people to actually see the film. A huge publicity and distribution machine is brought to bear on convincing people they need to see yet another American film. There is absolutely no way in the world that an independent filmmaker can compete with the firepower of a studio in terms of putting their actors or their actresses on the front of a magazine, on trailers, in TV spots and print ads in magazines and newspapers. It's a losing battle.

It's rather like politics. If we're honest, there's not much point bitching about Tony Blair and what a mess it all is unless you're prepared to put your money where your mouth is and say, 'Okay, I don't really *want* to, but I'll engage myself in politics, in order to change something I really don't like.'

Alternative Distribution

An alternative way to proceed is to use the Internet, which is an incredibly effective tool. Another option is to come up with an alternative to what we call a cinema. This is something that I've been trying to preach for the last five years. There is absolutely no reason why the bricks and mortar and red seats of a movie theatre need to be the definition of what is a cinema, full stop. A cinema is any space where chairs can be placed all facing in the same direction; where a white wall or a screen exists; and where a medium-priced digital projector is connected to a tape or a DVD or even a computer with a couple of speakers. *That* is a cinema.

In a way, this takes us back to the roots of cinema and a

time when it was brought to the small towns and villages of Italy by a van. A projector and screen were set up, possibly outside, and a pianist was brought in to play accompaniment to the images. Now we can do that ourselves and with an image of very high quality. So cinema can function in much the same way as theatre. Since 2000 I've been doing 'live' mixes of *Timecode*. This involves a limited amount of equipment but it allows me to re-mix my film in front of an audience, thus turning the film into a living thing rather than the projection of something finished and dead. A system for doing this did not exist at that time, but I knew that the technical requirements were fairly straightforward – it was merely a matter of putting certain items together. And everything worked fine. I'm surprised we don't see more of this kind of improvisation.

Until quite recently, good-quality digital projectors were more expensive than film projectors, so one could understand why cinema-owners were not prepared to invest that kind of money in technology that, without a doubt, was going to change in eighteen months. You'd have an obsolete piece of equipment on your hands. But the quality of digital projectors is going up and the price is coming down, as is the size of the projectors. So a cinema could really be anything. It could be a nightclub, it could be a temporary building that you acquire for six months and which functions as a cinema. And the base of that cinema exists on the Internet, in the sense that all you need to do is go on a website to find out where that cinema is going to have its venue for the next six months. The biggest problem is one of attitude.

This is a problem that applies particularly to distribution, but also more generally to the revolution in digital cinema-making, to the issue of Hollywood-versus-indie, and to the aspirations of most filmmakers. I would guarantee that if you scratch most filmmakers and ask them what their aspirations are, the majority will say, if they're being honest, 'Hollywood.' The reasons are obvious: they can earn much more money, they can be more famous, and they can be part of a more exclusive club. Their lifestyle aspiration – their *romantic* aspiration – is epitomised by the myth of Hollywood. Having spent time in Hollywood and seen other filmmakers and how they can live, I can see the appeal. But at the same time it's a bit like a pact with the devil. My agent said at the time, 'The problem with Mike is that he doesn't understand the Los Angeles social contract.' I agree. I didn't, and I don't. The social contract runs something like this: 'I will buy a house in LA. I will abide by the rules of the LA community. I will not argue with the studios. I will embrace the good life here above all else. I will not mention Godard or other such directors as a reference to anything in Hollywood . . .'

Those who aspire to Hollywood do so for essentially financial and social gains. And I would say that, as with any kind of interesting art movement, the avant garde or cutting edge of cinema will be the minority who, if you scratched their arm, really aren't interested in those aspirations. And it's those people at whom this book is aimed.

So I would urge and encourage filmmakers interested in digital filmmaking to form their own clubs and their own forms of distribution, in much the same way as, for example, in the pop music industry there are independent website-based record companies who sell their music exclusively through the Internet, not through conventional retail sources. That suggests that there is more solidarity on the cutting edge of the music industry than there is in the film industry. It would take – it *will* take – some considerable effort to organise a strong enough distribution system. But it is already starting to happen. The Film Council and various independent industrial factions are setting up digital cinemas across Britain, and that definitely is the future. There's no point arguing about it.

What I think we need to avoid is the prospect of the digital distribution world becoming just a new territory for the conventional studio base. Although the studios are very slow to read the writing on the wall, they are now seeing the folly of their ways and are trying to muscle in and colonise aspects of progressive digital media – because they know it's the future. Just as Kodak is dropping the production of film and concentrating all their effort on digital media – because they still want to be Kodak, just as Paramount still wants to be Paramount.

Coda

What's now happening is a kind of rethink. As the professional cameras are getting smaller, the domestic cameras are getting a little bit bigger. I believe the design will meet somewhere in the middle. The camera will be of a size more appropriate to our bodies, our hands, how strong we are. We'll come to the same conclusion as the manufacturers of the better stills cameras. If you look at a Nikon or a Leica or a Canon, you see an object which, ideally, you would use two hands to hold, so making it more stable; which your fingers can fit round comfortably but don't dwarf; which has buttons and controls that are big enough for your fingers to operate cleanly and for your eyes to see without wearing very thick glasses.

Recently, there has been a phenomenal rise in two things: first, in the quality of mobile phone cameras, and second, in the intense competition between mobile phone manufacturers, which means that every time they come up with a new phone they have to come up with a new range of gimmicks for it. They'll do anything – personal organisers, stills camera, a *movie* camera. People are now recording their daily lives on mobile phones and transmitting them to each other. So that's the latest gimmick. But I've noticed more and more that people seem quite happy with the quality of stills they're getting on their mobile phones – and one can see how, almost accidentally, the evolution of the camera into the mobile phone is something that could quite comfortably happen. If you buy a digital stills camera now, it's almost certain that you'll have the ability to record movies as well. So in the last couple of years the division – it used almost to be a sacred barrier – between a stills camera and a movie camera seems to have completely vanished. And I see no reason why the quality of images on mobile phones won't radically improve in the next eighteen months as better chips are used.

Recently, I had the opportunity to look at the new Sony High Definition camera, and it's the size of what would have been a smart domestic camera. Something that's entirely portable. The picture image quality is superb, broadcast quality. Suddenly you're arriving at the kind of proportions and flexibility of equipment that people were talking about as a fantasy only twenty years ago. It's the kind of camera you need to support on your shoulder, and quite heavy. It's perhaps twelve inches long, so big enough to need the use of two hands and therefore out of the danger zone of wobble. Plus, because it's a professional camera and we're all snobs, we tend to treat professional equipment with a lot more respect than we do so-called domestic equipment.

* * *

Having just proof-read these pages, I'm struck by the sense of how quickly things are moving along in the world of technology. I'm now testing new cameras from Panasonic and Sony, one of which records directly on to a drive. In other words, tape will shortly disappear as the main recording base. Picture and sound quality are improving while prices are dropping, and the gap between what used to be pro and amateur is narrowing yet further. Camera design is becoming more practical, but it still has a way to go – there is still a lamentable lack of dialogue between the designers and the filmmakers themselves. I'm itching to design one myself, a camera that would be 100 per cent practical. The 'Fig Rig' that I designed to support the new cameras and reduce camera-shake is doing well and I get encouraging feedback from people who have used it, which makes me think that it was a step in the right direction. Certain cameras that I refer to within the book are already out of date (such as the PD-100), but the practical information will always be valid.

One new innovation has highlighted a psychological problem which is worth addressing here at the very end of this book, and that is *virtual storage*. We are using the word 'virtual' more and more in the context of the brave new digital world. What it seems to mean is 'there, but not there.' All information is becoming computer-based, stored on drives and discs. Once tape disappears, there will be no tangible physical evidence of what we do. I have to say I still like that physical basis of my work. If I want to find something, I look in a list, I locate a tape, I put it into a machine, and there is my footage. But things are going to be very different now.

My footage will live on a drive which can only be accessed via a computer. I will never see my footage as an object – a can of film, a tape in a case, a reel of sound, a negative of a still image. Those formats are all poised to disappear. This makes me feel insecure, and I have resorted to spending days making back-up copies of all my information. I have had no choice but to become an obsessive filing clerk. I make three copies of everything I generate, and then I deposit each of the three at a different location. Why? Because, in my deeply superstitious pagan mind, I have the notion that otherwise *it could vanish without trace.*

This is the new reality – it's virtual, man, get with it. Cinema is dead, long live cinema.